PRAISE FOR *THE GLOBALLY MOBILE FAMILY'S GUIDE TO EDUCATING CHILDREN OVERSEAS*

"Never before in history have parents faced so many choices on how to best educate their children. For globally mobile families, the number of factors to consider in choosing a school is amplified.... Finally, help has come! Wrobbel describes all options clearly, listing the benefits and challenges of each so parents can make well-informed choices. I highly recommend it!"

—RUTH E. VAN REKEN, COFOUNDER,
FAMILIES IN GLOBAL TRANSITION

"We needed this book fifty years ago. When our family moved from the USA to Nigeria, the topic most hotly debated among parents was education of children. We needed this book to calmly and objectively point out the advantages and challenges of each option.... I highly recommend this book and wish Wrobbel had written it earlier."

—JAMES E. PLUEDDEMANN, PROFESSOR OF INTERCULTURAL
STUDIES, TRINITY EVANGELICAL DIVINITY SCHOOL

"Wrobbel provides invaluable information, insight, and counsel for globally mobile families considering the education of their children overseas.... Karen draws on critical research, collective wisdom, and professional and personal experience to provide a definitive educational guide for globally mobile families."

—DAVID A. WELLS, FOUNDER, PRINCIPAL, AND EXECUTIVE
CONSULTANT, GLOBAL SCHOOL CONSULTING GROUP

"For expat parents, planning for the education of their children is an important and complex task. Wrobbel helps families consider appropriate goals for the education of their third culture kids given cross-cultural considerations *and* the individual needs of their children. . . . I would highly recommend this book to any parents embarking on an overseas assignment."

—MELISSA SHIPMAN, EXECUTIVE DIRECTOR, THE PROFESSIONAL ASSOCIATION OF CROSS-CULTURAL CONSULTANTS IN EDUCATION (PACE)

The Globally Mobile Family's Guide to
Educating Children Overseas

The Globally Mobile Family's Guide to
Educating Children Overseas

To Joanne,
with appreciation for your
friendship

Ka Wrobbel

KAREN A. WROBBEL

WIPF & STOCK · Eugene, Oregon

THE GLOBALLY MOBILE FAMILY'S GUIDE TO EDUCATING
CHILDREN OVERSEAS

Wipf & Stock
An Imprint of Wipf and Stock Publishers
199 W. 8th Ave., Suite 3
Eugene, OR 97401

www.wipfandstock.com

PAPERBACK ISBN: 978-1-6667-1021-2
HARDCOVER ISBN: 978-1-6667-1022-9
EBOOK ISBN: 978-1-6667-1023-6

09/16/21

To my husband, Paul, and daughters, Beth and Rebekah.
Together, we were privileged to enjoy twenty
memorable years as a globally mobile family.

Contents

Contents

Acknowledgments

THIS BOOK BENEFITS FROM many people's years of work with globally mobile families. I acknowledge in particular my colleagues at SHARE Education Services, the Intermission MK Education Consultation (IMKEC), and Interaction, International, who freely share ideas and expertise with one another for the good of the families we serve. Beyond my reading and research, much of what I know about the education of globally mobile families comes from the shared pool of wisdom among these colleagues. Whenever possible, I have tried to cite individuals, but there is a lot that we all know for which we cannot identify a specific source. Please know that I appreciate you and am thankful for our partnership together in working with families.

I am also thankful for my faculty position at Trinity International University, where research and writing are expectations of the job, and I can therefore carve out time to work on a project like this. Though it has taken several years due to the other demands of the position, this book is the fruit of hours in the library or behind a closed office door (with thanks to Margie for helping "guard" it to keep me undisturbed). Thank you to my colleagues who have encouraged me along the way and asked about progress on the book. The staff at Trinity's Rolfing Library have been incredible, fulfilling my multiple requests for interlibrary loans and helping me track down some obscure resources.

Thank you to Wipf and Stock for your commitment to publish books based on the value of the content. This book is for a highly specialized audience and you were willing to put it into print even though it is not destined for a best-seller list. I and the families and organizations who will benefit from it are grateful.

My husband, Paul, has supported me completely at every turn of this project (and in every other aspect of life in our 44 years of marriage). He encouraged me when the going was tough and cheered with me when Wipf and Stock offered the contract. He has taken on more at home so that I could write and didn't flinch too much when I told him about the auxiliary costs of the project. In every way, he has been and is my biggest fan and supporter, and I am grateful for his unfailing partnership in this and every other endeavor.

1

So You're Moving Overseas

IF YOU'RE READING THIS book, my guess is that your or your spouse's boss has called you or your partner into the office to say something like, "We need someone in our South Africa office and I think you are the person for the job." Or perhaps it's that orders have come through for your next assignment as a military member and that is a posting at Rota, Spain or Subic Bay in the Philippines. Maybe you sought the international life by joining the diplomatic corps, a mission, or some other non-governmental agency. Whatever the path that has brought you to the place of an international move, your life is about to take, or perhaps already has taken, a turn to the global. As you prepare to live outside of your homeland, you need to consider how you will educate your children in your new country of residence.

For us, the global life started with a college experience. My husband and I both played in our college's concert band, and one summer, the band toured Venezuela, playing concerts throughout the country. We had new experiences, met interesting people, and began to gain an appreciation for another way of life. Among the interesting people we met were North Americans and other ex-patriates living in Venezuela, people who had chosen to live and work among the people mostly as missionaries, though we also met folks who were employed by the oil companies. That trip sparked our interest, which led to deeper exploration, and eventually to us joining a mission agency to work as missionary teachers who taught the children of other expatriate families overseas. That band tour started a journey that included twenty years of international residence in three different countries. We also raised our daughters internationally, moving overseas when the youngest was just four months old; they each returned to the US to start university at age eighteen.

Whether you have chosen to move overseas like we did or have been asked (or mandated) to do so by an employer, there is a lot to think about with an international move. The employee will think about the work assignment: the challenges and opportunities it may bring, and ways to prepare to be successful professionally in the new role. The employee, the spouse, or both will think about the logistics of the move: finding a place to live, what to take and what to store, and how to educate their children. This book focuses specifically on that final aspect of the move. The various education options all have benefits and potential limitations. Further, sometimes what is seen as a limitation by some may be perceived as a strength by others. One reason for the differences in perspective on the available options is that people differ in their expectations for and views on the purpose of education. These purposes and outcomes are discussed in chapter 2. Later chapters explore the various options one by one, with a general overview, description of benefits and potential limitations, and discussion of other considerations. Each chapter closes with questions for further reflection and resources for further information.

Why is a book on educating globally mobile children necessary? In the homeland, choosing the means of a child's education is relatively straightforward. Most parents[1] will choose the local, government-run school. Some will opt for a private school[2] that meets specific needs or desires of the family, such as religious education or an academic or artistic specialization, and still others will choose to teach their children at home.[3] In general, though, decisions in the

1 About 90 percent in the US. "Back to School Statistics."

2. In the US, 8.3 percent of the population chooses private schools. Ryan et al., *Those Who Can, Teach*, 321.

3 About 2 percent of the US population (two million of seventy-six

homeland are based on well-known considerations and experience with the educational system, possibly including family tradition or other factors. In a global assignment, all is new and unfamiliar. The options used by others in your company or organization may be the "go to" option for many. These default options may also be what is recommended by human resource departments. Educational reimbursement policies of the company may also reflect these preferred or default options. However, given the range of choices that are available and the different circumstances of every globally mobile family, parents need to carefully weigh the options, using as much information as available, to make the best decision for their own family in their specific circumstances.

Making a careful and appropriate choice for the children's education can be critical to the success of the global assignment, so companies also benefit from supporting and facilitating choice as much as possible. The adjustment of the expatriate employee's family, including the children's education, directly impacts the employee's adjustment and related success in the global assignment. For example, Kang summarizes, "The results showed that children's education had a significant positive relationship with overall adjustment and each of the subsidiary variables of expatriate adjustment. Notably, *children's education predicted both the general environment of expatriates and host interaction of expatriates better than work adjustment of expatriates.*"[4]

Children (including their educational needs) were the number one reason for premature departures from global missionary assignments, according to the 1996 attrition study by the World Evangelical Fellowship.[5] This study of workers from fourteen nations explored the reasons for premature departures from work as missionaries and considered solutions that might help reduce what they called "undesirable attrition."[6] The study underlines the importance of a successful transition for the children in order for the

million) are homeschooled. "More than 76 million"; Ryan et al., *Those Who Can, Teach*, 375.

4. Kang, "Community and Family Factors," 94–95 (emphasis added).

5. Brierley, "Missionary Attrition," 92.

6. Taylor, "Prologue," xiv.

family to successfully complete the international assignment. Stanley Davies, writing about attrition from a UK perspective, notes that "children's needs, especially education, become more pressing as secondary school approaches";[7] and Belinda Ng, representing the viewpoint of what they called "new sending countries," stressed that "Asian parents are concerned about their children losing their identity and mother tongue," especially if they attend international schools. She stresses the importance of addressing the issue with "concrete actions" lest "fewer families . . . present themselves for service, or we will be raising a new generation of Westernised missionary kids."[8]

Some believe that the best way to educate globally mobile children is in a way that is as close to the homeland as possible. For example, Drake advises, "Repatriation is facilitated by an overseas education which closely parallels US education. Assess the curriculum overseas by how well it will fit in upon repatriation."[9] While there may be benefits to an educational approach that is close to one's homeland and it may aid in repatriation, an education that tries to reproduce the homeland in the international context will miss benefits that come specifically by being in a global setting. These benefits may include an expanded worldview, experiences with other societies, cross-cultural skills,[10] and the opportunity to learn one or more additional languages with an authenticity that cannot be achieved in a homeland classroom. While some of these benefits can be realized even if the child is in an educational setting that is like the homeland, some of them cannot, or they cannot be experienced with the same depth because it is the very interaction with the other societies that brings about the benefits of a globally mobile childhood.

While a full discussion of how your child will be impacted by your decision to live internationally is beyond the scope of this book, it may be helpful to overview what Pollock, Van Reken, and

7. Davies, "Attrition," 156.

8. Ng, "Reflections on Pastoral Care," 283.

9. Drake, *Educating Children*, "Background on Teen Repatriation Problems."

10. Pollock et al, *Third Culture Kids*, 139–151.

Pollock call the "third culture kid experience."[11] They use the term "third culture kid" to describe globally mobile children, but there are various terms used, so perhaps a place to start is by defining terms and categories. The term "third culture" was coined by researchers who learned that people who lived outside of their home culture combined elements of the first, or home, culture with elements of the host, or second, culture into a new, society-linking third culture.[12] The definition has progressed over time but the key is that it is an "interstitial culture," with "shared commonalities of those living an internationally mobile lifestyle."[13] Some have objected to the term "third culture kid" because it seems too much like "third world," which may be viewed as pejorative, so other terms are used to describe the experience of individuals who fill these important roles that link peoples and societies. Besides third culture kids (TCKs), the children of globally mobile parents may be called "global nomads,"[14] internationally mobile children, or transnational kids. Ruth E. Van Reken suggests the term "cross-cultural kids" as a descriptor that focuses specifically on what the child experiences, not the parents' choices.[15]

As the parent's employment affiliation is part of the identity of a globally mobile employee, their dependent children may also be described by their parent's employment affiliation. They may be called missionary kids (MKs), military kids (or the less-kind "military brat"), biz kids, or diplomats' kids. The family affiliation will influence the international experience.[16] For example, military families often live on a military base in the overseas location that may be a lot like "home." Missionary families generally live in the local community, learn the language, and often stay in a country for many years. They tend to have close and long-term relationships

---

11. Pollock et al, *Third Culture Kids*.

12. Useem et al, "Men in the Middle," 169–79.

13. Pollock et al, 17.

14. Schaetti, 'Global Nomad,' para. 2.

15. VanReken, "Cross-Cultural Kids," 33.

16. For an expanded discussion of the impact of affiliation, see "Organizational Sub-cultures: The Impact of Affiliation" in McCluskey, *Notes From a Traveling Childhood*, 9–13.

with host-country citizens and the local culture. Diplomats are typically rotated on a regular basis.[17] Living in an expatriate "bubble" feels more like "home" but insulates expatriates from the local society. This can be positive and/or negative, depending on one's goals and perspective.

Living internationally will change you and your children. Ruth Hill Useem and Ann Baker Cottrell write about adult third culture kids (ATCKs), the former "kids" who find themselves still viewing the world differently as adults. In her research, Useem learned that adult TCKs often experienced "delayed adolescence," or a sense of being out of sync with their age group due to their different experiences. They also struggle to fit in, especially as they try to discern the unwritten behavioral norms in a new location. This "new" location can include their home country, which helps explain the title of the entire collection of essays, *Strangers at Home.* Useem and Cottrell also note that these internationally experienced individuals tend to have high educational and career achievement.[18]

Both adults and children can anticipate an expanded view of the world as a result of living internationally. Things that seem far away and perhaps even unimportant take on heightened importance to people who have lived in the region or who have a broad sense of the world's interdependence. The significant changes that have occurred in Venezuela over the past twenty years are of great interest to me because I first lived in Venezuela in the early 1980s, when the currency was a stable 4.28 *bolívares* to the US dollar, there was development due to oil wealth, and the country was one of the more stable democracies in Latin America. We lived there again in the late 1990s when Hugo Chávez was elected president and watched firsthand as some of the changes he implemented began to move the country in a socialist direction. Now we live in the US, but we still follow Venezuelan news closely because of the people we know personally whose daily lives are impacted by events there.

My sense of patriotism is different after living abroad. I remain a person who loves and appreciates my home country, but living in

17. An interesting memoir of one family's life in the US diplomatic corps and their varied postings around the world is LaTurner's *Voluntary Nomads.*

18. Useem and Cottrell, "Adult Third Culture Kids," 26.

other places has helped me see that there are other ways to do things and we may not be the best in the world in everything. (Sorry if that offends some of my fellow US citizens.) I have a greater passion for diplomatic relations and for finding peaceful, collaborative solutions. Perhaps some of that would have come with age regardless of residency, but I believe that knowing and having friendships with real people in other places has had a significant influence on my view of the world.

One characteristic that differentiates expatriates from immigrants is that globally mobile families usually expect to eventually return to their home country. For some, life overseas may be a specific assignment of just one or two years followed by repatriation to the homeland. Other expatriates live internationally for many years, even longer than our twenty-year international sojourn. One outcome of the globally mobile lifestyle may be that your children choose to make your adopted homeland their home as adults and/ or they marry someone of another nationality. Neither is necessarily bad or good, but it may surprise you to think about this possible outcome. I was unprepared for the question when my minister's wife in Spain asked me if I would object to our daughters marrying Spaniards (they were very young at the time), and it made me think deeply about my expectations and my relationship to my new country of residence. Though many of my former students (I was a teacher in international schools) have returned to their passport countries for their adult lives, others have chosen to remain in the country where they were raised or to live and work in a third country, thereby continuing the expatriate lifestyle.

How will a globally mobile lifestyle impact your children and you? McCluskey lists six "gifts" that globally mobile parents give their children. These include "deep understanding and tolerance for differences" as they interact with many cultures and different kinds of people, "a broader vision" of the world, and "comfort communicating with adults" because of the opportunities and necessity they have had to do so.[19] Additional benefits McCluskey describes include their "commitment to community or social service," "greater

19. McCluskey, *Traveling Childhood*, 26–28.

comfort with diversity," and "closer family ties," since the "family is the only consistent unit that moves through time and place, the family members are thrown back on one another in a way that they are not in a geographically rooted situation."[20]

Pollock, Van Reken, and Pollock include an entire chapter on the benefits and challenges of a globally mobile upbringing. However, their treatment of these benefits and challenges recognizes that the benefits have shadow sides, like the two sides of a coin. For example, while a globally mobile child has an expanded worldview (McCluskey's "broader vision"), they also have confused loyalties in areas such as politics and patriotism. A global upbringing enriches them culturally, but they may not know much about their own culture. Finally, the Pollocks and Van Reken describe the "three-dimensional" view of the world that TCKs possess, having experienced the world in tangible ways. However, they also have a "painful view of reality" because of those close interactions with other societies.[21]

This realistic perspective that recognizes distinct benefits as well as challenges in a globally mobile upbringing forms the outline for *Unrooted Childhoods: Memoirs of Growing Up Global.* The essays that make up this book are written by adults who grew up "global." They are organized into four sections: enrichment (recognizing benefits), estrangement (descriptions of losses and pain that come from a global upbringing), rootlessness (the challenge of home being everywhere and nowhere at the same time), and identity (wrestling with the question of who am I and where I belong). The book's opening essay, "Living in the Transit Lounge," captures the idea of being an "intercontinental wanderer" whose home is in that transit lounge.[22]

As noted earlier, a complete discussion of the benefits and challenges of a globally mobile upbringing is beyond the scope of this book. However, now having highlighted some of those areas, with references for further reading if you want to learn more, I turn

20. McCluskey, *Traveling Childhood*, 26–27.

21. Pollock et al, *Third Culture Kids*, 139–51.

22. Eidse and Sichel, *Unrooted Childhoods.*

back to the theme of education specifically, and what the global lifestyle may mean for your child's education, the focus of this book. Though written with a focus on tertiary education, Carroll identifies several things that can be helpful in thinking about education in the international setting.

- Your kids will be characterized by *educational mobility*, "moving across national boundaries, often from familiar to unfamiliar learning settings."

- They will experience *pedagogic variation*, referring to "the fact that people teach and learn in different ways and hold different underpinning values and beliefs about education."

- If English is not the primary language of the child or family, *learning in English* will become an issue if the child attends an English-language school.[23]

No matter which educational option you select, your globally mobile student will need to adjust to new settings. Carroll further identifies the adjustments that may be necessary for students.

- Make sense of new academic assumptions and expectations. There may be different standards for what makes work "good," and students may encounter unfamiliar practices.

- Deal with language issues.

- Learn via different teaching methods. They may find it difficult to gain information from lectures, seminars, and tutorials; and they may or may not feel free to speak up.

- Mix and collaborate. Globally mobile children will need to build relationships with other students and/or feel "able to bring their own knowledge, skills, and experiences into interactions and to have their input heard and valued by others."

- Find support and guidance. Students will need to determine how to get help and direction in the new setting.[24]

---

23. Carroll, *Tools for Teaching*, 17–18.
24. Carroll, *Tools for Teaching*, 18.

Going global is both exciting and challenging. For families with children, identifying the best educational option for their children, given their circumstances and the available options, is a major decision with significant implications. In the short term, the adjustment of the children can make or break an international assignment. In the longer term, realizing the maximum benefit of a globally mobile upbringing while mitigating as many limitations as possible is the significant challenge for parents. The next chapter will lay a foundation for decision-making through a discussion of educational goals and philosophy followed by the implications goals and philosophy have on educational decisions. This will be followed by chapters that each look at one educational option, identifying benefits as well as potential limitations and other considerations for decision-making.

2

Intentional Planning for Children's Education Overseas

WHEN WE FIRST MOVED overseas many years ago, we were full of anticipation and eager to encounter new experiences. We moved to Central America to study Spanish, and with complete confidence in our agency and colleagues, took the advice of others who had gone before us regarding living arrangements, household help, and education for our children. We enrolled our preschool children in the *guardería* (nursery) at our language school, and, thankfully, were very happy with the loving care they received there while we struggled with vocabulary, pronunciation, and the subjunctive tense. Admittedly, that was before information was so widely available on the Internet. But nevertheless, we took the advice of others without independently informing ourselves and then making intentional choices based on that information. I'm glad it worked out for us. Others are not necessarily as fortunate.

Today, Internet searches and virtual or actual visits are normal steps in planning an international move. Plenty of information is available. However, families may still rely on the advice of others as they choose educational options. That's not a bad approach. "Listen to advice and accept discipline," recommends the writer of the biblical proverbs.[1] Others in your company or agency who have lived

1. Prov 19:20.

where you are going understand the challenges and opportunities, and can speak from their firsthand experience. It is wise to listen to their advice.

However, I caution you to not stop there. Each family is unique. Your family has values that may not be shared by your coworkers. You may have aspirations for your children that are different than the aspirations of your colleagues. Your children may have special gifts that you want to nurture or needs that must be addressed. I urge you to go beyond the advice of others to examine the available information to make the best decision for your individual circumstances, values, and priorities. This book will help you do that.

In this chapter, we focus on intentional planning based on your educational goals and values, so that you can make informed and deliberate decisions for your children's education. Intentional decisions are possible only when you have clarified your long-term goals and values. In later chapters, we will explore the various options that may be available in any given location so that you can apply what you know about your goals and values to selecting the most appropriate educational option for your children.

Option selection includes identifying the available options, weighing pros and cons, and counting the costs of an option: financial, personal, and opportunity.[2] For example, families may prefer an international school within a reasonable commute from home that is taught in their home language and follows the curriculum of their homeland. However, that might not exist in every situation, or if it exists, it might not be within their budget. Families may find that the time it takes to commute to and from a preferred school is excessive, or that the preferred option, such as homeschooling, may negatively impact their work because of the time it takes. Intentional decision-making requires considering these multiple factors and then selecting the best choice within your constraints.

---

2. Opportunity cost is an economic term, referring here to opportunity(ies) that may be missed as a result of a decision. It represents the trade-offs when, in order to get one benefit, you may have to give up something else.

IDENTIFYING EDUCATIONAL GOALS

One of the seven habits of highly effective people is to "begin with the end in mind."[3] Intentionally planning for children's education requires thinking about the end goal. What do you want education to accomplish in and for your child(ren)? What is the purpose of education? What outcomes do you desire? Take a moment to pause and think about these questions. If you can, discuss your responses with your partner. You might find that you do not come up with the same answers!

On the surface, asking what the purpose of education is may seem like an easy question. But as Sloan has noted, "you might have better luck asking, 'what is the meaning of life?'"[4] Educational philosophers and practitioners suggest different purposes of education, and these understandings of education's purpose differ among societies and cultures. Parents, too, have different expectations of education. The 2016 Phi Delta Kappa poll of the public's attitudes toward the public schools reported that "fewer than half of Americans (45%) view the main goal of public education as preparing students academically; the rest split between a focus on preparing students for work (25%) or preparing them to be good citizens (26%)."[5] Views on the purpose of education have also changed over time. In the following paragraphs, I will highlight historic developments in education to illustrate various views on the purpose of education. This will not be an exhaustive discussion of educational history or philosophy, but it should be sufficient to help you think about your goals for your children's education.

Prior to the emergence of writing systems, learning took place exclusively at home and in the community as children learned fundamental life skills such as hunting, fishing, preparing food, etc. from their parents, extended family, and community. Though not necessarily formal education, the goal of education was to **prepare children for life and the world of work** as practiced in their society. Similarly, the more formal system of apprenticeships, which first

3. Covey, *7 Habits*, 96–144.

4. Sloan, "What Is the Purpose," 7.

5. "Why School?," 7.

appeared in the Middle Ages,[6] prepared individuals for the world of work. (Apprenticeships are still used today to prepare individuals in certain vocations.)

Gene Carter, the former executive director and CEO of the Association for Supervision and Curriculum Development (ASCD), writes that today, "schools must be preparing children to compete in the global environment."[7] Being prepared to compete includes work skills and the so-called twenty-first-century skills.[8] Goals of this education would be "creating communicative, imaginative, tech-savvy, multilingual students who are prepared for jobs that do not yet exist."[9] This approach is a modern version of the goal of preparing children for the world of work. Proponents believe that education should prepare students to earn an income. Scott Walker, the former governor of the US state of Wisconsin, was in the headlines when he suggested that the mission of the University of Wisconsin be changed, replacing "search for truth" and "improve the human condition" with "meet the state's workforce needs."[10] This view focuses specifically on the business of earning a living and minimizes learning for learning's sake. Reagan reports that this is also the case with the non-Western societies he studied."[11]

However, even when societies are preparing students for the world of work, the emphasis can vary and result in different outcomes. Reagan writes, "In modern capitalist societies in general, and in American society in particular, educational institutions are often expected to *serve the needs of the economy* (or, more accurately, of employers) rather than the needs of individual workers . . . In the cases examined in [Reagan's] book [on non-Western education], the emphasis placed on vocational preparation is largely an *empowering one, with greater emphasis normally placed on the*

6. "Apprenticeship," line 18.

7. Carter, "Purpose of School in the 21st Century," lines 14–15.

8. Battelle for Kids. "Partnership."

9. Carter, "Purpose of School," lines 23–24.

10. Strauss, "Purpose of Education," lines 2–3.

11. Reagan, *Non-Western Educational Traditions*, 249.

needs and aptitudes of the individual rather than on the needs of the employer."[12]

Related to the goal of preparing children for life and the world of work is the idea of education's purpose being to **develop the intellect and prepare students for life in general**, not preparation for a specific vocation. As early as the seventeenth century, the Czech John Comenius promoted compulsory education for all. His goal was that all children would learn "all the subjects of human concern."[13]

A related, though distinct, purpose of education is the idea that education is to **train and prepare for citizenship**. However, this idea of education for citizenship also means different things to different people. The idea of education for citizenship may be traced to Plato's *Republic,* where Plato proposed "an ideal state characterized by unity and harmony."[14] The unity and harmony could be achieved by people *knowing their place* and *willingly subordinating themselves* to the state.[15] People would do what they are "best fitted to do," which leads to a division of labor where there are workers, soldiers, and philosophers (the rulers).[16]

Plato's view is quite different than a modern perspective of education for citizenship. John Dewey, for example, also believed that education should prepare students for citizenship, but to him it meant citizenship in a pluralistic society, "with disagreement and diversity as a corollary to freedom."[17] Jeffreys highlights how the goal of preparation for citizenship can mean very different things in different circumstances. He points out that "in democracies the prevailing view is that education . . . should produce people capable of thinking for themselves and dedicated to truth wherever it is to be found. In the dictatorships the function of education is rather to

---

12. Reagan, *Non-Western Educational Traditions,* 250 (emphasis added).

13. Compayré and Payne, *History of Pedagogy,* 128.

14. Brown, *Aims of Education,* 2.

15. Brown, *Aims of Education,* 2.

16. Brown, *Aims of Education,* 3.

17. Brown, *Aims of Education,* 5.

stamp all citizens with the orthodox political doctrine."[18] Reagan notes that what might be called "civic education," or education that prepares one for citizenship, is a "broadly shared concern" among many non-Western educational traditions. His study, which included societies in Africa, Asia (Confucian, Hindu, and Buddhist traditions), the Middle East (Islam), Europe (the Rom, or gypsy, population), and indigenous people of the Americas, found that "in every case . . . there is a concern with helping children grow into the kind of adults who will function effectively and appropriately in their society."[19] These approaches are all preparation for citizenship, though the outcome of each can be quite different.

Horace Mann led the movement in Massachusetts to provide free, compulsory schools for all children. His vision of education was also related to citizenship, with a focus on **education for democracy**; he believed that "a republic cannot long remain ignorant and free."[20] He explicitly emphasized that this free public education should be "free of sectarian religious influence" and should be for "children of all religious, social and ethnic backgrounds."[21] By 1918, all children in the United States were required to attend at least elementary school.[22]

John Dewey and education progressivists recognized that education would include specific skills such as reading, writing, speaking, and calculating. However, they emphasized that education should not be just about content but should instead teach students how to learn. Their goal for education was for students to **achieve their full potential and then use their skills for the greater good**. This approach sees education's task as **equipping individual students to fulfill their self-selected destinies**.[23]

Another view of education's purpose is **socialization** of children according to the norms of the society. At times, this is an

18. Jeffreys, *Education: Nature and Purpose*, 14.

19. Reagan, *Non-Western Educational Traditions*, 249.

20. Cremin, "Horace Mann," line 69.

21. Cremin, "Horace Mann," lines 75–77.

22. Watson, "How Public Schools Work," lines 29–30.

23. Thomas, *International Comparative Education*, 26.

explicit goal. In other cases, it may be in the "hidden curriculum" (learning experiences that are not explicitly stated in the formal curriculum). This is closely related to the goal of citizenship; perhaps some would consider it synonymous. As children attend school, they learn to get along with others and relate to classmates and educators who may hold different perspectives than those held in their family. Unwritten rules of societal behavior are reinforced or taught. Nations, and even parts of nations, share certain common values, and these are passed along in schools as part of the socialization process. Thomas calls this "producing good people."[24] National heroes, for example, are celebrated, and children learn the society's values from their examples. In the United States, there is the well-known though likely apocryphal story of George Washington chopping down a cherry tree. When questioned about it, Washington reportedly replies, "I cannot tell a lie," and confesses to the tree-chopping.[25] The nation's first president, a national hero, teaches children the commonly held value of truth.

In the international setting, parents may wish to carefully consider the values and society into which their child will be socialized at school. Typically, a school will prepare its students for citizenship in the country where it is located or, in the case of international schools, of the predominant culture or culture on which the curriculum is based. If a parent has specific goals or expectations in this area (for example, either to prepare their children for citizenship in the home country, or to prepare their child for citizenship in the host country), they will want to think about how schooling will socialize their child. Even if a parent chooses a so-called international school, there will still be socialization based on the norms of one or more countries. Some schools explicitly indicate the society upon which the education is based, such as "The American School of [city name]" or "The British School." Parents who choose a host-country school for their children's education can anticipate that the child will be socialized in the cultural and societal patterns of that nation. Parents can anticipate explicit and "hidden-curriculum"

24. Thomas, *International Comparative Education*, 26.
25. Richardson, "Cherry Tree Myth," lines 1–11.

socialization into the norms of citizenship for the country upon which the education is based. This will be discussed further in the chapters on the various educational options.

Globally mobile kids overseas differ from immigrants, since they and their parents presumably will retain their home-country citizenship and anticipate eventual return to their homeland. However, as newcomers who are learning the ways of a different country, globally mobile kids have similarities to the immigrant population, and parents can learn from writings about immigrants. There are educators and policymakers who believe that it is especially important for immigrant children to be part of local schools so they can assimilate into the society by learning the behavioral norms and values of the majority culture. This reason is sometimes used to suggest that missionary kids, for example, whose parents want to develop close relationships with the local population, should attend host-country schools. However, one of the reasons parents may choose homeschooling is to limit their children's interaction with these other perspectives and instead inculcate the parents' deeply held values through education in the home.

Yet another perspective is that "the primary task of formal education is to **develop the intellect**."[26] Some (e.g., Hutchins[27]) believe that students should learn from a set course rather than being free to learn what they like. In this view, students should learn "the collected wisdom of the ages" and "sustain the great intellectual tradition."[28] Another way to state this perspective is that its goal is to promote a goal of "well-informed people who understand the physical and social universe."[29]

Finally, **education for the purpose of spiritual development** can be traced from early human history. The Bible records God telling the Jewish people to take the words of God's law and "impress them on your children. Talk about them when you sit at home and when you walk along the road . . . Write them on the doorframes

---

26. Brown, *Aims of Education*, 35.

27. Hutchins, *Higher Learning*, 59–87.

28. Brown, *Aims of Education*, 35.

29. Thomas, *International Comparative Education*, 26.

of your houses and on your gates."[30] Further, Moses adds, "When your son asks you, 'What is the meaning of the stipulations, decrees and laws the Lord our God has commanded you? Tell him [about God's deliverance]."[31] It was the church that kept learning alive in Europe during the Middle Ages through cathedral schools, from which the university developed.[32] In the United States, the 1642 "Old Deluder Satan Act" was prompted because the religious Puritans wanted to ensure that people could read Scripture (to fight that old deluder, Satan) and be good citizens. This groundbreaking law required children to attend school. By 1647, towns with more than fifty households were required to appoint a teacher, and those with one hundred or more were required to set up a grammar school.[33]

Many faiths have traditions of religious schooling, including the Christian-school movement, parochial Catholic education, and other religious schools. These schools typically follow the locally or nationally designated curriculum with the addition of religion classes. In Protestant Christian schools, such as the international Christian schools that may be available to your children overseas, faculty go beyond simply adding Bible classes and chapel by seeking to permeate the study of all subjects with a biblically based worldview and integrating principles of the Christian faith into all instruction. This would include, for example, asking about a character's motivations and traits in light of scriptural standards when studying literature, and including religious events and context when studying history.

This integrative approach is not unique to Christian education. Muslim education also seeks to "remove the dichotomy of religious and secular education systems" and create "the good and righteous man who worships Allah, . . . and builds up the structure of his earthly life according to the Sharia (Islamic law)."[34] Zaki Badawi points out that "Muslim educators unanimously agree that

30. Deut 6:7–9.
31. Deut 6:20–24.
32. Gangel and Benson, *Christian Education*, 109.
33. "Massachusetts School Law," lines 12–20.
34. Jamjoom, "Foreword," v.

the purpose of education is not to cram the pupil's minds with facts but to prepare them for a life of purity and sincerity."[35]

Parents with strong religious beliefs, including missionary parents, will want to be sure that their children develop a worldview based on their faith perspective. This can be accomplished through various means. For some, the option of a faith-based school may be available, where their children will have teachers and even classmates who share their faith. Others may choose to homeschool to ensure their children are educated in agreement with their faith commitments. Others may use public or non-religious private schools and prioritize religious teaching at home. All parents with deeply held faith commitments should carefully examine the explicit and hidden curriculum of any educational option they consider in light of their faith so that, rather than confusing children with teaching that opposes the parents' deeply held convictions, children's developing faith can be appropriately nurtured.

This very brief history of education highlights some of the purposes of education. It also illustrates why it is not a simple matter to identify the purpose or purposes of education, since societal needs, perspectives, and interests vary widely.

OTHER GOALS FOR GLOBALLY MOBILE CHILDREN

Beyond the broad educational goals detailed above, expatriate families need to consider other potential goals related specifically to their globally mobile experience. As introduced in the first chapter, the child who is raised in a global setting will be changed by virtue of that experience. Therefore, parents need to consider how the international experience will and could impact their child, consider any hopes or goals that they have, and plan accordingly. A colleague and I developed the following list of goals for globally mobile children when I was coordinating children's education worldwide for a non-governmental agency with workers who resided internationally over extended periods of time. I have adapted them for

---

35. Zaki Badawi, "Traditional Islamic Education," 104.

application to the various types of expatriate families (business, military, diplomat, missionary).

First, the education option selected for a globally mobile child's education should provide for **healthy development** in all areas: academically, emotionally, socially, physically, and spiritually/morally. While this may appear to be obvious, healthy development merits inclusion because some international postings may present challenges to one or more areas of healthy development and parents need to identify this as a goal and work toward fulfilling it. For example, children have reported bullying or favoritism because of their expatriate status.[36] Bullying can happen anywhere and it is never desirable. In the international context, parents may need to reevaluate educational options if the child is being bullied because of nationality. On the other side of the spectrum, parents may need a strategy to address the situation of the child who develops a high view of herself because she is favored at school due to nationality or appearance. Families with strong spiritual or religious values may find some locations particularly difficult because of the difference in and pervasiveness of religious values, and may want to consider the location's impact on their children. Though complete physical safety can never be guaranteed (there are auto accidents, for example, in the homeland), Donald and Margaret Grigorenko focus on places that may pose specific risks and may not be family friendly.[37] Some employers or sponsoring groups consider this (such as when the military deploys only the member and the family remains behind), but regardless of the sponsoring agency's actions, families need to consider the level of risk that is acceptable to them.

Living internationally offers children an opportunity to learn about another culture or cultures. A second worthy goal is that globally mobile children **appreciate, understand, and thrive in the cultures in which they live.** By "cultures," I specifically mean the home, host, and third culture. When I refer to home culture, I mean the country of the family's passports, and/or the place where they started and eventually anticipate returning. For a family preparing

---

36. Wrobbel, *University-Level Academic Success,* 145–147.

37. Grigorenko, "Experiencing Risk," 25–44.

to leave their homeland for a first overseas assignment, such as the business person assigned to an overseas posting, identifying the "home" culture is probably straightforward. However, this is more complex, for example, when the parents are from different passport countries and they are already living in a third country, preparing to move to a fourth country. Further, answering the question of where home is gets harder the longer a family lives overseas. Let's agree that it's complicated but use the definition that passport country equals "home" to get to the point of the educational goal. The host culture is the "overseas" place where the family is temporarily living as expatriates. Again, this can be complex, especially with families who reside in one place for so long that the "overseas" residence no longer feels temporary. In this case also, though, I ask the reader to note the complexity but use the term as defined for this discussion. The "third culture" is the culture of internationally mobile people, who "live among nationals of another society and interact with them in common enterprises. These are the men-in-the-middle . . .who connect two or more bureaucratic structures."[38] The idea of third culture and the concept of third culture kids was introduced in the first chapter and will continue to be referenced in later chapters. It is thoroughly developed in Pollock, Van Reken, and Pollock's book *Third Culture Kids: Growing Up Among Worlds*.

For this discussion of educational goals, I suggest that it is ideal if the internationally mobile child can go beyond her home culture to learn about and appreciate the host country and its culture. In some circumstances, the only host-country nationals the children ever know are their maids, gardeners, and drivers, which leads to a limited view of the country and its people. This, in my opinion, is unfortunate. I acknowledge that opportunities to interact with the host culture may be limited by security measures or other lifestyle choices. However, if possible, the child (and parents) will be enriched by appreciating, understanding, and even learning to thrive in the host culture. This may include some level of language learning, having friends from the host culture, and general participation in the life of the community rather than limiting

38. Useem, "Interfaces," 130.

oneself to an expatriate bubble. The children of missionaries or other NGO workers are often best positioned to achieve this goal in comparison to other expatriate groups (such as business, military, or diplomats' kids) because of their closer contact with host-country citizens. However, *any* expatriate can take steps to understand and appreciate the host culture if it is a value. One thing that can help with appreciating, understanding, and thriving in the host culture is learning the language. Consider whether you have hopes, aspirations, or expectations about language learning for your child. Is it your goal or hope that your child(ren) learn to communicate using the host-culture language? Would you consider fluency in the local language to be a desirable goal, and what means would you consider to accomplish that goal? These are important questions to answer with your partner.

As you consider the importance of your child appreciating, understanding, and even thriving in the home, host, and third cultures, another question to discuss is the importance to you that your child(ren) identify your home culture as their home culture. If your overseas assignment is relatively temporary, such as a two- to three-year business posting with a return to the homeland to follow, this question is likely moot. However, for families who will live internationally for a longer period of time, this is an important consideration. "Where is home?" can be a complicated question for third culture kids, and—though your home will likely be some combination of home and host cultures—parents need to determine how closely they wish to identify with the host culture and the implications that may have for their children. Further, if the parents are from two different passport countries, will one or both of those cultures be the primary focus of your home, or will you focus on the host country or some combination of cultures in the home?

A further culture to appreciate, understand, and thrive in is this society-linking, multinational culture that is shared among others with the similar experience of residing in a country other than one's home country. There is a commonality of experience with others who have lived outside their homeland, even if the individuals have not lived in the same country. Understanding, appreciating, and thriving in this society-linking "third culture" can be a valuable outcome of an internationally mobile childhood, as individuals with social and cross-cultural skills, flexibility and adaptability, and linguistic skills are and will likely continue to be in demand in the global economy.

A third expatriate-specific educational goal would be to find a **healthy balance between the parents' commitment as workers and the commitment they have as parents.** This goal is perhaps relevant to all parents everywhere (how do you find work/life balance?), but for globally mobile families, the blend between the job and personal life can sometimes be blurred. The work may be noble—supporting one's nation (such as diplomats or members of the armed services), serving people in need (diplomats, charitable workers), or sharing one's faith (missionaries). Because of the importance of the work, people can be so highly committed to the work that they neglect their families. It is especially challenging when both parents are involved in the work, such as is likely the case with missionaries or other charitable workers.

Work/life balance can also get out of whack the other way, with too much focus on family life. This can happen when one or both partners spend a lot of time on children's education and as a result, do not make satisfactory progress in their work. For example, missionaries generally invest significant amounts of time and energy to learn the local language(s) because they need the language to achieve the goals that brought them to the international location. If one parent, often the mother, does not learn the language because she is homeschooling the children, her longer-term ability to live and minister in the community may be hindered. An appropriate goal would be to find an educational option that works well for both the children and the parents, ensuring that the children receive the education they need while enabling the parents to accomplish their work.

Academic aspects are another consideration. Unlike immigrant families, who anticipate becoming permanent residents in their new country, expatriate families generally (though not necessarily) plan to repatriate to their homeland at some time in the future. If this is the case, I urge parents to **seek educational options that meet or exceed their homeland's educational standards.** Each country has its own expectations for educational achievement, and if and when children return to their homeland, they will be expected to know and be able to do the same things as their homeland peers. In many cases, educational differences between national systems are not a matter of better or worse but simply are different. However, if parents decide to use an option that does not meet or exceed their homeland's standards, the parents will need to develop and implement a plan to compensate for these differences or deficiencies. This will be developed further in the chapters that address the various educational options.

Do you place a priority on children receiving an education that offers technology and other resources that are similar to your homeland? Additional resources might include opportunities for Advanced Placement (AP) courses or vocational training. Do you want an option that has multiple "tracks" available so that there are options such as university-preparatory and vocational paths? Is it your expectation that all or most of your child(ren)'s teachers be from your home country, or is this not important to you? Is it a priority for your child(ren) to be in class with age- and grade-level peers? Some families may need special education services, and finding an option that meets these needs will be a priority. (See later chapter on special educational needs.)

Post-secondary education is another consideration for expatriate families. Do you anticipate that your child will engage in post-secondary education, and do you assume that will be university? If you are assuming your child will attend university or want to be prepared for the possibility of your child attending university, is it important to you that your child(ren) be prepared to enter higher education in your home country, or would university entry in another place be acceptable to you? Further, while university is an assumption for some families, others may anticipate options such as vocational preparation or direct entry into the work force. Assumptions about what happens after secondary school need to be examined so that the student's studies will keep the desired option(s) available.

A final consideration in the intentional selection of an educational option is a **healthy social and emotional life for the child**.

Some educational options may have a negative impact on the child's emotional or social well-being. When families are placed in remote locations where few educational options exist, they need to ensure, as do the agencies that assign them to the location, that they will be able to adequately care for the developmental needs of their children. While it is educationally possible to homeschool or take online classes from a remote location, the lack of friends can be a significant detriment, especially to teens who are at an age where the peer group is increasingly important.

INTENTIONAL PLANNING BY
CLARIFYING PERSONAL VALUES

Individuals and societies reach different conclusions regarding the purpose or goal of education. Similarly, individual perspectives on educational values vary. Parents may find that even they and their partner hold differing assumptions regarding educational expectations and goals. While these differences may not surface in the homeland, the different expectations can trigger disagreement or even conflict when the complexities of an international move come into play. Ideally, each parent will consider their own education values and goals, and then the two will discuss their values and goals to choose the best option for their child(ren) in their specific location.

There is no one right, universal answer to the question of the purpose or goal of education. For parents who are moving overseas, the question is even more complex and requires careful thought to ensure that an educational option can achieve their goals for their children's education. The following chapters will examine various options individually to help parents be informed of advantages, potential limitations, and longer-term implications of the alternatives. Armed with appropriate information, parents can make intentional decisions to accomplish the educational goals they have established for their children.

QUESTIONS FOR DISCUSSION
AND REFLECTION

1. What is the purpose of education?
2. Has my perspective changed from my initial response early in the chapter now that I have read the entire chapter?
3. In what ways might my view of the purpose of education influence my educational decisions for my children during my overseas sojourn?

3

International Schools

INTERNATIONAL SCHOOLS ARE THE default choice for many expatriate families, especially those in the business or diplomatic communities. These schools, often with names like The American School of [City Name] or The International School of [City Name], can be found in many places around the world. They generally offer an excellent education and are staffed by well-qualified teachers. Many international schools follow the curriculum of the International Baccalaureate, which is a recognized credential for university admission and one that can lead to advanced standing at some universities.[1] In their review of parental priorities for selection of international schools, MacKenzie, Hayden, and Thompson point out that "with the increasing globalization of business and its associated mobility of employees and their families, the numbers of privately funded 'international schools' worldwide have grown."[2]

POSITIVES OF INTERNATIONAL SCHOOLS FOR GLOBALLY MOBILE FAMILIES

One benefit of international schools is that it is easy for students to transfer among these schools because of their similar educational

1. Learn more about the International Baccalaureate at www.ibo.org.
2. MacKenzie et al., "Parental Priorities," 300.

approach. Families that anticipate a limited stay in a country find that international schools are desirable because of the consistency among these schools, especially among those that use the International Baccalaureate (IB) program. Skelton reports that many children are in a given international school for just two to three years as parents change positions.[3] MacKenzie, Hayden, and Thompson's research supports the idea that consistency, and the IB specifically, is an important factor in families' choice of option: "It would appear from the responses of these parents that the existence of the IB Diploma program was an important factor in their choice of school . . . None of the three schools [studied] offers alternatives to the IB Diploma itself, or the more respected concept of a respected university entrance qualification, which attracts the parents."[4]

A further reason why international schools are often the default choice of globally mobile families is that the schools are either like their homeland or have "international" credibility. This includes international credibility for university admission. In describing the rationale for creating the IB program, Hill writes, "The need for an internationally recognized diploma was also an important motivating force for parents and teachers. It would serve as an international passport to higher education and therefore facilitate global mobility."[5] Many, though not necessarily all, parents of globally mobile children anticipate that their children will return to the parents' homeland for university, and an IB diploma can be interpreted appropriately by educational authorities in the homeland. Even if parents do not necessarily prefer that their children return to the parents' homeland but are open to them studying in another nation, the International Baccalaureate is recognized by many countries as a high quality, college-preparatory secondary education.[6]

English is often the language of instruction in international schools. This suits North American, British, Australian, New

3. Skelton, "Defining 'International,'" 41.

4. MacKenzie et al., "Parental Priorities," 311.

5. Hill, "History of International Education," 19.

6. "Country Recognition Statements."

Zealander, and other English-speaking families, since their children can enter school in the new location without any linguistic challenge. For those whose home language is a language other than English, English-language schools can be perceived positively by parents who want their children to speak English well due to its status as an international language, since their children can develop high levels of spoken and written fluency in English through the international school experience. When writing about factors influencing parent choice of international schools, MacKenzie, Hayden, and Thompson write, "It would be difficult to misinterpret the apparent importance of the English language to these parents. Repeatedly it emerges as one of the crucial factors in parents' choice of school and is frequently cited as the single most important . . . English is the main attraction [of international schools]."[7] The English used in an international school is typically American or British English, though students may encounter other world Englishes through their teachers and classmates.

In some locations, there are international schools conducted in languages other than English, such as French or German. Curriculum will generally follow that of the language's home country (i.e., France or Germany). Choosing one of these schools can be a benefit to citizens of those countries who want their children to be educated in their own language. Alternatively, education at one of these schools may offer the benefit of learning an additional language for speakers of a language other than the language of the school. I know of a North American, English-speaking family that sent their children to the German school in Madrid, because they were planning to relocate to Germany at the end of their assignment in Spain. Experience with English at home, Spanish in the community, and German at school helped these globally mobile children become trilingual.

Classmates at an international school are likely to be from a variety of countries, including the host country.[8] Some will be

7. MacKenzie et al., "Parental Priorities," 311.

8. Understanding the experience of host-country citizens in international schools is beyond the scope of this work, though an interesting and worthy topic for inquiry. One study of interest in this regard is Tomoko Wakabayashi's

long-term residents of the host country, while others will be posted there for just a year or two. The students who are host-country nationals will typically be from only the wealthiest of the country's citizens due to the cost of international schools. Some students will be native speakers of English (or the language of instruction at the school), while others will be speakers of other languages who are learning and using English in their education.

In some locations, families can find international Christian schools. This subset of international schools offers a Christian religious education for families who want their children to receive a faith-based education. Like international schools in general, international Christian schools typically provide an excellent education; many offer Advanced Placement (AP) courses, as well as other international exams like the British International General Certificate of Secondary Education (IGCSE). Some international Christian schools are affiliated with the IB program.

Because international schools serve a globally mobile population, they may play a significant role in helping families transition to a new location. McLachlan's research was based on a Personal Social Education (PSE) program at the international school where she worked. She writes, "The international school community serves as a safe haven, a place for families to root for a few months or many years depending on the family's circumstances. Specifically, international schools meet the needs of [internationally mobile] families by increasing their security, decreasing some of the feelings of transience, and encouraging a sense of belonging to help them survive and thrive in an [internationally mobile] lifestyle.[9]

POTENTIAL LIMITATIONS

Given all these benefits, you may wonder why any globally mobile family would *not* choose an international school education for their children. There are several reasons, which may or may not apply to your situation.

thesis.

9. McLachlan, "Global Nomads," 172–73.

One, if not the most, significant reason to opt for a choice other than the international school is cost. International schools are simply very expensive. The schools are generally privately run and not financed by government subsidies, so all costs need to be paid by student tuition and fees. Parents can expect to pay fees that may be comparable to university fees in the US. In addition to tuition, some schools charge a lump-sum capital fee to help fund buildings and other capital improvements at the school. This lump sum may be the same whether the student is enrolled for a year or for the entire primary and secondary schooling experience. For the children of international businesspeople and diplomats, payment of school fees is often part of the benefit package for an international assignment, and therefore, the high cost may not be a factor. Middle-class families who would not typically be able to afford the tuition and fees of an international school are able to benefit from the school when the costs are paid as part of the employee's relocation package. For families who are paying the fees themselves, however, the cost of an international school may be prohibitive. Costs may be lower at international Christian schools, especially for families engaged in religious work. In some cases, schools are able to offer discounts to religious workers if the workers' sponsoring organization participates in the running of the school (sharing costs and responsibilities) and/or if teachers fundraise all or part of their salary/living expenses.

Another potential limitation to selecting an international school has to do with you and your child's relationship to the host culture. In the first chapter, I asked readers to consider their goals for their child's education and suggested that a benefit of an international assignment that families might want to embrace would be learning another language and getting to know another culture. For families who move every year or two, this may not be practical, but for families who anticipate a longer sojourn in a particular location, learning the language and culture could be excellent benefits for the children. In an international school, it is likely that world languages will be part of the curriculum. However, the language of the place where the school is located may or may not be taught in the school. Additionally, children in an international school may not be motivated to learn the local language when they can use English to communicate with classmates.

A further aspect of relationship to the host culture that is a potential limitation of selecting an international school is who your child's friends are likely to be. Classmates at the international school will include a diverse group of students from many nations, which can be a benefit to your child. However, the other side of that benefit is the potential of limited contact with a range of people from the host culture. Classmates from the host culture are likely to be limited to only the wealthiest of the host country due to the high costs of school, as discussed earlier. In some places, international students' contact with the host culture could be only with those wealthiest families at school and then with those who are tending to your needs, such as maids, gardeners, and drivers. If you value learning about and connecting with the host culture, these potential limitations need to be considered. At the end of the day, you may still find the international school to be the best option for your child. However, you may want to seek ways for your child to have positive regular contact with the host culture and language in order to take advantage of the unique language-learning opportunity afforded by international living.

OTHER CONSIDERATIONS

Parents may be unfamiliar with the world of school accreditation, but it takes on significance when selecting an international school. Accreditation is a process of quality assurance and continuous improvement, and it includes the requirement that the school meet a set of standards, verified by a process of peer review. If you choose an international school, be sure that it is accredited by a recognized agency. One is the Council of International Schools (CIC);[10] others include the Western Association of Schools and Colleges (WASC)[11]

10. Council of International Schools, https://www.cois.org/.

11. Western Association of Schools and Colleges, https://www.acswasc.org/#!.

and Cognia (formerly AdvancEd).[12] Verify that the school is accredited by not only checking the school's website but also by visiting the web page of the accreditor to ensure that the school remains accredited and in good standing.[13]

If you have a child with special learning needs, you will want to carefully explore what the school offers. As noted earlier, international schools are typically funded by tuition and fees, and they may not provide the special education services that government-sponsored schools in the homeland are able to provide. This is not to say that all schools do not provide services. It is simply a caution to make sure you find out what is available and whether it will meet your needs. This includes evaluating physical accessibility for students with mobility needs, since all locations may not have awareness of and sensitivity to the needs of those with limited mobility. Parents should check well in advance if special educational services are required by a member of the family to see what is offered by the school. Chapter 9 provides further discussion of special educational needs in the globally mobile context.

Many schools offer services for speakers of languages other than English (or the language of the school). However, those services are not necessarily available at all grade levels. For example, English as a Second Language (ESL) services may only be offered in the early primary grades. After that, the school may require students to be able to demonstrate a set level of English proficiency in order to enroll. These policies are based on the school's mission, constituency, and available resources for providing services.

Within the genre of international schools, you will find that there is choice among international schools in some locations, but in other locations there may only be one international school. If there is more than one international school, you will want to carefully evaluate the options to see which seems to be the better fit for your student. When we lived in Caracas, Venezuela, there were two major international schools, and we made a point to evaluate both before deciding on an option for our daughter's education. This

12. "Find Accredited Institutions."
13. "What Does It Mean," lines 18–26.

included visits to the schools, conversation with administrators, reading the schools' printed and online materials, and talking with others in our organization who were already living in Caracas and who knew something about the two schools. Though both had excellent teachers and a solid curriculum (including the IB program), we found subtle but significant differences in the "feel" and culture of the schools, and that was important as we selected the school she would attend.

A further potential limitation of international schools is that "schools designated as 'international' may not meet the needs of all [internationally mobile] parents of diverse cultures. Henry (1996, 94) notes, '. . . even if diversity and cultural pluralism is evident in the school, schools can still effectively be alienating places for many students and parents whose cultures are different from the one celebrated in the school.'"[14] For example, in a school that is called "international," the primary culture among the students may be a North American (US) culture or a British culture. Parents of that culture may feel at home and know the unwritten cultural "rules," while parents of other nationalities may not feel comfortable. One cultural difference may be related to parental involvement at school. Some cultures view the school and home as separate domains (e.g., Sweden, Denmark, Finland, Holland, Italy, France), so these parents are unlikely to be involved at school. Lack of involvement at school, however, does not mean the parents are not involved in their children's education. McLachlan notes that "these parents were involved in their children's education directly 'at home' and indirectly through their parenting practices."[15] Parents from these cultures may not understand or feel comfortable with requests for room mothers, party assistance, or other parental involvement at school.

Parents who do not speak English (or the school's language of instruction) well may also feel excluded at the international school. I have worked in English-language international schools with a high percentage of Korean students. Though the schools welcomed

14. McLachlan, "Global Nomads," 176.
15. McLachlan, "Global Nomads," 196.

parent involvement, we found it difficult to involve the Korean parents. Though there were also cultural factors, the language level of the parents was a significant challenge to their interaction at the school. As schools, we had to take initiative to discover meaningful ways for these parents to be involved and to communicate appropriately with them.

One last consideration for parents considering the international-school option is understanding and evaluating the entire concept of "international school." First, it is important to understand what exactly constitutes an international school, which may not be as simple as it sounds. Then, parents need to decide whether or not an international education is even important to them. I caution parents to not discard the idea of "international education" too quickly, thinking it unimportant and instead seeking an education just like back home. In MacKenzie, Hayden, and Thompson's research, they found parents were divided in their desire for "international" education; it was important to some but not an important reason for all respondents to choose the school. Interestingly, though, they found that some of the parents who did not view it as important initially came to value it later.[16] Finally, parents need to determine whether the international school they are considering actually meets their definition and expectations of an international school.

To unpack these steps, it is important to define "international education" and what it is that a truly international school does differently than a school that is not "international." Schools base their "international" moniker on various criteria, and this list is not necessarily comprehensive:

- their student body comes from many nations, and/or
- their faculty come from countries other than the host country, and/or
- their faculty comes from many nations, and/or
- the school is located in an "international" location, such as a school that follows the British national curriculum but is located in Kenya, and/or

16. MacKenzie et al, "Parental Priorities," 311.

- the school curriculum[17] is intentionally international in focus.

Those who specialize in and research international education would focus on the final point: intentionally international in curricular focus. Hill reports that the "first known definition of international education devised by a group of school representatives from different countries meeting together" identified the following as an international education:

> It should give the child an understanding of his past as a common heritage to which all men[18] irrespective of nation, race or creed have contributed and which all men should share; it should give him an understanding of his present world as a world in which peoples are interdependent and in which cooperation is a necessity. In such an education emphasis should be laid on a basic attitude of respect for all human beings as persons, understanding of those things which unite us and an appreciation of the positive values of those things which may seem to divide us, with the objective of thinking free from fear or prejudice.[19]

The preceding definition reflects the idea that the founders of the international-schools movement and the International Baccalaureate (IB) were interested in promoting world peace and international understanding.[20] Further, they noted that students were being prepared for national university entrance exams in small groups largely by nationality, leading to "unviable class sizes and cultural isolation."[21] The combination of their goals for promoting

17. Curriculum refers to the course of study—the teaching and learning experiences, both planned and unplanned. It does not refer to the textbooks, which instead are a resource to support the curriculum.

18. Though gender-inclusive terms are appropriately used today, the author has elected not to change or insert "sic" into quotations from earlier works when the use of "man" to represent people (e.g. mankind for humankind) was considered appropriate.

19. "Course for Teachers Interested in International Education," 1950, cited in Hill, "History of International Education," 22.

20. Hill, "History of International Education," 19.

21. Hill, "History of International Education," 202.

international understanding and the practical need for classes of a sustainable size for the schools' economic health contributed to the development of international schools and the International Baccalaureate.

Today, Gellar suggests the term "internationally-minded" might be a more useful approach.[22] In this framework, an internationally minded school would be distinguished by an educational curriculum that emphasizes world history, literature, and cultures, stresses the interdependence of nations and peoples, and de-emphasizes the study of topics from the perspective of only one country or group of countries. Additionally, these schools would be distinguished by an ethical aim to "actively espouse and uphold certain 'universal' values and to make them an integral part of the life of the school, its community, and, particularly, the children in its care."[23]

However, others do not define "international education" based on an international curricular focus. For example, the fourth point on the preceding list—the school is located in an "international" location—seems to be the perspective of the Hong Kong Education Department. In a 1995 working-group report on the provision of international schools, the Hong Kong Education Department defines international schools as those which "follow a non-local curriculum and whose students do not sit for the local examinations (i.e. Hong Kong Certificate of Education Examination). They are operated with curricula designed for the needs of a particular cultural, racial, or linguistic group or for students wishing to pursue their studies overseas."[24] This definition of international schools may serve for this government agency to distinguish types of schools more than to define international education, but it does offer an example of this definition.

As a consequence of these different perspectives on what constitutes an international education, Wilkinson's caution is wise: "It is important to examine, on a school-by-school basis, what the school

22. Gellar, "International Education," 31.

23. Gellar, "International Education," 31.

24. "Report of the Working Group on the Provision of International School Places," quoted in Bray and Yamato, "Comparative Education," 54.

means when it decides to call itself 'international.'"[25] MacKenzie, Hayden, and Thompson make a similar point, writing, "Particular problems for parents, in trying to exercise choice in the context of such schools, may be posed by the fact that the term 'international school' is not, in itself, any guarantee of a particular ethos or philosophy of education, and by the wide variation which exists in the nature of such schools around the world."[26]

This chapter has overviewed the benefits, potential limitations, and other important considerations for globally mobile families who consider an international school for their children's education. I urge you to review what you identified as the purpose of education and the outcomes you desire in light of these factors as you consider the possibility of choosing an international school for your globally mobile child's education.

The question of what constitutes an international education, and whether or not parents want that for their children, goes back to the discussion in chapter 2 about informed and intentional decision-making. Having decided to use an "international school," parents then must discern what the school means by that title, whether that is the kind of education the parents want for their child, and then whether the school carries out that stated purpose in practice.

Finally, consider the words of this international-school administrator, who states:

> I sometimes tell parents that they enroll their children at an international school at their peril. The children will be learning different things in a different way from anything in their parents' experience. The values they learn may not be identical to their parents' values. Children may change. They may become independent. They won't just be the same Japanese or Arab children who have learned to speak English. They will become a mix of nationalities. That is what makes it so hard for the parents.[27]

25. Wilkinson, "International Education," 187.

26. MacKenzie et al., "Parental Priorities," 300.

27. McLachlan, "Global Nomads," 167.

The entire experience of being a globally mobile family will impact children, and regardless of the schooling option selected, children may change. They will become independent and they will have very different experiences from their parents. International schools can be an excellent option to help children grow in those new ways and thrive in their international location.

QUESTIONS FOR REFLECTION

1. How well does an international school meet the goals and fulfill the purpose(s) of education that I identified in chapter 2? Are there any goals for my/our child's education that would not be met in an international school, and if so, what will I/we do to address that, if anything?

2. If you have considered one or more specific international schools already for your children, think about what they mean when they describe themselves as international: Does that perspective of international education align with what I/we desire for my/our children?

4

Host-Country Schools

YOU MIGHT BE SURPRISED at the inclusion of a chapter on host-country schools in this book, since globally mobile families may initially consider international schools or other options and not think about the host country's schools. Though perhaps less frequently used by globally mobile families, host-country schools are an option that merits consideration and that may be appropriate for or even beneficial to families in some situations. Missionary families especially, who generally stay in a country long enough to learn the language well and to integrate deeply and develop a close connection with the host culture, find the host country's schools to be a good option in some situations.

This chapter may also be of interest to families for whom English is not the home language. The Korean student who enters an English-language school in Germany, for example, may experience many of the benefits and potential limitations that I describe here related to host-country schools, even though it is not a host-country school. This could include Korean families in the US on temporary or semi-permanent assignment. Kang reports there are at least 119 Korean multinational corporations in the United States registered with the Korean Chamber of Commerce and Industry in the USA; there were 323 companies registered in 2008, prior to the economic downturn.[1] Park and Abelmann note that parents are eager for their children to learn English because "English represents class mobility, often signaling entrance into, or maintenance of, a higher class level in South Korea. English is also the tool of striving to participate in a cosmopolitan world. Therefore, it is not surprising that US-based expatriates utilized the expatriation period for their children's exposure to English education. This action links to Korea's recent globalization policies emphasizing English education to elementary students. Mastering of English is regarded as 'an index of cosmopolitan striving.'"[2] Whether in the US or in a third country, Koreans—or students of any nationality—may choose an English-language school to achieve these linguistic benefits.

POSITIVES OF HOST-COUNTRY SCHOOLS FOR GLOBALLY MOBILE FAMILIES

Children who attend host-country schools are able to live at home and participate in normal family life. Parents have day-to-day interaction with their children and continue speaking into their children's developing identity, character, and values. Additionally, relationships among siblings continue within the family home. For globally mobile families, the family unit is one of the few constants among all the changes brought about by this lifestyle, so the benefit of being at home cannot be overstated.

In addition to living at home and participating in normal family life, the children are able to be a part of local community life. Within the local community, children can have a high level of interaction with the host culture, which can lead to cross-cultural understanding and competence as children develop friendships with classmates.[3] In my research, Diana (a pseudonym) said that French school "got [her] into the culture full-fledged; all [her] friends were French girls and French guys."[4] Heather felt her host-country school

1. Kang, "Community and Family Factors," 6.
2. Park and Abelmann, "Class and Cosmopolitan Striving," 650.
3. Pollock et al, *Third Culture Kids*, 153–65.
4. Wrobbel, "University-Level Academic Success," 133.

experience helped her "to be able to really understand German and really get involved," and Priscilla, who attended host-country schools in Poland, described host-country schooling as "an incredible opportunity . . . to learn the culture, learn the people, and learn positive traits about the culture."[5]

Though this depends on the location, parents may find that the educational level of the host-country schools is as high or higher than in the homeland. I am acquainted with North American families who used French schools for their children's education. These families took French homeschool materials with them on their home leave to the US so that their children would not fall behind academically in the French system. Parents should expect to find differences in when and how certain content is presented, but the rigor of the education and its standards may be comparable to or even higher than the homeland.

One of the potential benefits of a globally mobile upbringing is the opportunity to learn one or more additional languages through formal study, informal interactions, or both. My own daughters (both now adults) speak Spanish fluently as a result of living in Spanish-speaking countries for the majority of their growing-up years. The Spanish they learned informally through community interaction and media was supplemented by formal classes in their English-language schools. Though only one of them currently uses Spanish in her career, they have both experienced benefits in cross-cultural understanding and the ability to communicate in Spanish for personal and professional purposes. When host-country schools are the educational option selected by a family, children will have an opportunity to learn the host-country language well. There are potential linguistic challenges for students in host-country schools, which I'll discuss in the next section. But for children who are at an appropriate age for an immersive language experience, or who have prior knowledge of the language, attending school in a second (or third) language can build skills in the language that will increase the student's connection to the host country, enhance understanding of the culture, and possibly be useful professionally later in life.

5. Wrobbel, "University-Level Academic Success," 132–33.

Another positive aspect of host-country schools is that they are likely to be convenient and inexpensive relative to other options. Though some globally mobile families are not concerned about the price tag because educational expenses are part of their benefits package, other families are responsible for children's school expenses (such as business people with smaller companies) or have limited employer benefits for school fees (such as missionaries; this may also include families who want an alternative to the "official" option of their sponsoring group). School fees and expenses vary by nation, but in general the government-run host-country schools charge low or no fees for education, even for expatriates in the country. A further benefit is that if the selected school is in the same neighborhood as the family's residence, it can be convenient for the family in terms of getting to and from school each day and for play-dates and other interactions with classmates outside of school.

POTENTIAL LIMITATIONS

Though there are benefits to using the host-country schools, there are also potential limitations that need to be carefully considered. I will talk about language first, since that is perhaps the biggest concern when considering host-country schools. However, even if the host-country school is offered in your home language, there are other potential limitations of host-country schools to consider, so please do read on.

The concern that likely comes to mind for most parents is the language difference. They wonder, for example, how their English-speaking child will adapt to a school where Italian is the language of instruction. Research on immigrant children's language experience is informative in this regard. In his research on language and cultural identify, Wakabayashi notes that "age and prior experience with the first language are crucial factors in second language acquisition."[6] The general consensus[7] is that the optimal age range for immersion

6. Wakabayashi, "Language and Cultural Identity," 21–22.

7. Note, though, that no one can "prove" anything in social-science research in the way that things can be "proved" in natural-science research.

into a second language for schooling is ages eight through twelve.[8] Students in this age group have had some schooling in their first language, creating a foundation upon which to build. Further, they have enough time remaining in school to develop proficiency in the second language. The second-best age is between five and seven years old. Children can develop conversational fluency quickly, and the academic demands of the curriculum are less intense than later (such as in secondary school). However, these younger children will not have developed a foundation in the first-language literacy yet.[9] Submersion into a second language for schooling after age twelve is generally not recommended because of the difficulty in keeping up academically while attempting to learn the new language.[10]

Elementary students are likely to develop conversational fluency quickly. This basic conversational language facilitates interpersonal communication (e.g., "Throw me the ball," "I'd like milk," "May I go to the restroom?") and can lead parents and teachers to think the child is "just fine" for schooling in the second language because she seems to be managing these interpersonal conversations well. However, research suggests that students studying in a second (or third) language will probably need academic support in that language throughout the family's stay in the host country. Further, it may take five to seven years or longer to develop age-appropriate mastery of the context-reduced, cognitively demanding language of schooling (academic language).[11]

If the family anticipates staying in the host country long enough for their child to be successful using the host-country language, there are still other important considerations. In the first chapter of this book, I challenged you, the reader, to consider the purposes of education from your perspective because identifying

8. See Collier, "Age and Rate of Acquisition" and "Synthesis of Studies."

9. Wrobbel, "When Should Children Start?," 4–7.

10. See Collier, "Age and Rate of Acquisition," 633; and Marsh et al., "Late Immersion," 302–46.

11. Conversational language is the context-rich language of everyday conversation. Academic language, however, is the context-reduced specialized language that is required for academic pursuits. See Cummins, "Conversational and Academic Language."

what you hope to achieve through education will help clarify benefits and limitations of the various options.

One purpose of education, especially in the public (government-sponsored) sector is preparation to be citizens of the nation. This purpose is fulfilled through explicit curriculum, where students are taught how government works in their country. Students learn patriotic songs; they learn about national heroes and the history of the nation from the perspective of that nation. This purpose is also carried out through what educators call the "hidden" curriculum: educational purposes that may not be intentionally stated (or even consciously targeted) but that nonetheless are taught through attitudes and actions. The hidden curriculum may include values, beliefs, and behavioral norms, and these may differ from those held by the parents. One student, Kathy, shared how she reverted to Japanese behavior without realizing it, even as a university student who had exited host-country schools eight years earlier. "I'm still very much Japanese, the way I relate to people, the way I communicate, the body language I use . . . As soon as I step out into the world [beyond my family that] I'm not as comfortable with, I begin to act Japanese toward them almost . . . [There are] cultural things that have influenced the way I behave."[12]

Culture will impact education in many ways. Brown appropriately notes, "A nation's cultural values are evidenced in their educational aims,"[13] and this is also evidenced by teaching philosophies and discipline methods. Brown cites the research of Geert Hofstede and others to make the point that "education and educational assessment are directly related to a nation's culture."[14] One area where cultural values are demonstrated is in whether students are expected to have an extensive knowledge base, or whether analysis and interpretation are considered more important.[15] Cynthia Storrs, whose children attended schools in Belgium, reports, "Often, teaching methods tend towards memorization rather than

12. Wrobbel, "University-Level Academic Success," 122–23.
13. Brown, "Cultural Dimensions," 68.
14 Brown, "Cultural Dimensions," 69.
15. Brown, "Cultural Dimensions," 70.

conceptualization . . . creativity is sacrificed for conformity, and analysis is less important than knowing the right answer."[16] It could be that your home culture similarly prefers memorization and conformity, so this would not be a concern to you. However, if you have different values, this may be an issue to consider. Culture is also evidenced in approaches to motivation. Matt Neigh, a TCK who attended host-country schools in a Western European nation for many years, remembers being brought in front of the class where he was "humiliated, slapped, punched or otherwise beaten for not being a good student."[17] The point is that a parent considering host-country schools will want to explore how the culture's values will be evidenced in schooling, including methods for classroom management and discipline, as part of a decision-making process. Additionally, parents need to evaluate their child's personality and how it fits with the culture's educational approach.

A final potential limitation of the host-country schools is that they may not adequately prepare the student for repatriation. This is an important difference between expatriates and immigrants. Unlike immigrants, expatriates anticipate repatriation, or return to their home country, at some point. Parents who consider host-country schools will need to consider the importance of repatriation. Would you be open to your child remaining in your host country for university and eventual career, or are you eager to ensure that your child be prepared to and desirous of return to your home country?

If repatriation seems many years away for your family, you might still consider the anticipated duration of your sojourn in a given country before your employer transfers you to a new location. A two-year experience in a host-country school may lay a foundation in a new language for your elementary-aged student that, if maintained, could lead to bilingual or near-bilingual fluency. However, the opportunity cost in academic development while focusing on language might be too great for your child, especially if the student is already in secondary school.

16. Blomberg et al., "Using the National Schools," 562.
17. Blomberg et al., "Using the National Schools," 562.

OTHER CONSIDERATIONS

If you consider the host-country schools, as with any option, parents must weigh the balance of benefits and potential limitations. Additionally, there are factors that are not necessarily a benefit nor potential limitation but that are still important to include in your evaluation of this option.

It is difficult to make broad statements about any country's schools that are consistently accurate because perceptions and realities within a country may vary widely. In Phi Delta Kappa's 2019 poll of the public's attitudes toward the public schools, only 19 percent of Americans gave the nation's schools an A or B grade (the top grades in the US system, where grades range from A to F, roughly indicating superior [A], above average [B], average [C], below average [D], and failing [F] achievement). However, 44 percent give an A or B to their local schools.[18] In the US at least, parents seem to think their local schools are doing well but are pessimistic about the nation's schools overall. This is illustrative of the challenges a parent may face when considering using a host-country school. You can learn about the nation's schools in light of their general characteristics, but you also need to investigate the individual school your child may attend. When we considered enrolling one of our daughters in a local school as a preschooler, I sought the advice of a trusted local friend who knew about the specific school we were considering to supplement the general understanding I had of schooling in Spain. Her insights were a key factor, though not the only one, in our decision-making process.

Among the important questions to explore is how local school leaders view having a foreign student in the school, and further, a foreign student who is still learning the local language. Similarly, understanding the classroom teacher's willingness to have an expatriate student in the class is essential. Neigh describes being ridiculed for being a foreigner and notes that when his parents complained to the school director about how he was being treated, they were told, "If you don't like the way we educate your son, go

18. "Frustration in the Schools," 21.

back to the U.S.!"[19] If the school is amenable to having a developing bilingual expatriate student, Storrs recommends seeking a "bridge" person who can help the parents and student understand the unwritten rules, such as "lunch money, bringing flowers at the end of the year, . . . expectations for birthday parties, and all the many other things that . . . are different" from homeland experiences.[20]

Your child may experience challenges, discrimination, or even favoritism because of her foreign status. Your child "may never be fully at ease in the national school,"[21] experiencing teasing or worse because of her (different) appearance, his limited language, or even your home country's foreign policy. Alternatively, your child may be *favored* in the host-country school because of appearance or perhaps the perceived status of your home country by the host-country citizens. Kathy remembers, "I was always different than the other kids. I was the only blond-haired kid. I was usually the teacher's pet. Even though I deserved punishment, like when I had done something wrong . . . the teacher would be really nice."[22]

If your child is enrolled in national schools for a number of years, such as may be the case with some missionaries' children, his opportunities for developing English (or other first-language) literacy and academic language may be limited. In this circumstance, parents need to make provision for ongoing development of first-language skills. Consider supplemental work in your first language at home. Some families accomplish this through regular "lessons" in the first language throughout the school year; others do more intensive first-language work during the summers. One university student at a selective US university who attended host-country schools through graduation from secondary school remembered that her parents did not provide formal supplemental education in English, but their home did have a variety of interesting reading materials in English. She credits her extensive reading in the first language (English, in her case) for her success in academic

19. Blomberg et al., "Using the National Schools," 564.

20. Blomberg et al., "Using the National Schools," 567.

21. Gieser, "Academic Stress," 18.

22. Wrobbel, "University-Level Academic Success," 145–46.

English.[23] That approach may be successful for the child who enjoys reading but may not be as successful for others, so parents are still urged to consider supplemental work in the first language.

Familiarize yourself with the school's educational philosophy, including classroom management, methods of instruction, homework expectations, and grading. As noted in the potential-limitations section, these areas can "have an enormous impact on children."[24] While the philosophy may be different than that to which you are accustomed, parents will need to discern whether that is simply one more difference in the international location to which you can adjust, or whether the difference is sufficiently negative to preclude the use of the host-country schools.

Host-country schools are a viable option under some circumstances for the education of globally mobile children. Benefits include language learning and enhanced cultural understanding, as well as the chance to live at home and potentially pay less than for other options. Parents are reminded that "education is . . . a carrier of the values of the culture of a society and as such these values are transmitted from teacher to student, from school to teacher and from educational system to school."[25] Students will pick up the values of the culture, and the influence of these values will be deeper the longer the student attends the local schools. Parents who choose this option will also need to identify ways to continue their child's academic development in the home language.

QUESTIONS FOR REFLECTION

1. How important is it to me and my partner for our children to share our cultural values and desire to eventually repatriate to our homeland?

23. Wrobbel, "University-Level Academic Success," 110.

24. Pollock and Van Reken, *Third Culture Kid Experience*, 218.

25. Brown, "Cultural Dimensions," 70.

2. How important is it to me and my partner for our children to know, understand and even thrive in the host culture where we live?
3. Which of the potential limitations are concerning to us, and how might we mitigate them if we were to use the host-country schools?

5

Homeschooling

HOMESCHOOLING HAS BECOME AN increasingly popular and accepted educational option within the United States. In 2012, the National Household Education Surveys (NHES) estimated that there were 1.8 million homeschooled children in the US,[1] and the National Home Education Research Institute estimates there are four to five million homeschooled students as of early 2021.[2] Internationally, numbers are more difficult to obtain, though Ray reports that home education is "on the rise in Australia, Canada, France, Germany, Mexico, South Africa, the United Kingdom, and Japan."[3] Though some US states and global countries may require homeschoolers to register in some way, "nearly a fourth of [US] states don't even require parents to notify anyone if they homeschool their children, much less offer any sort of verification that they are doing so."[4] Further, some homeschool families may prefer to be "off the radar,"[5] making the actual number of homeschoolers

1. "Homeschooling," line 1.
2. Ray, "Homeschooling: The Research," line 1.
3. Ray, *Worldwide Guide*, 7.
4. Kunzman, *Write These Laws*, 2.
5. Tara Westover's *Educated: A Memoir* shares her experience as a homeschooler in a rural community in Idaho with parents who wanted to limit connection to the government. While her experience is not necessarily normative, it is illustrative.

difficult to determine. Conservative Christians are the largest subset of homeschoolers in the US, according to most experts, but homeschool advocacy organizations "serve almost every demographic imaginable."[6]

In describing homeschoolers, Brabant notes:

> Home schooling is present on all continents and its diffusion is increasingly facilitated by modern communications technologies. Its value is debated in both the academic literature and the popular press. The debate is largely centered on political, social and moral issues such as the formation of citizens, parental and children's rights, the value of schooling, the evolution of educational institutions, the transmission of values and the moral development of the child. While research on the practice is limited, available evidence to date suggests that home schooled children perform as well or better than their schooled peers in terms of academic and social outcomes.[7]

Note Kunzman's description of the debate surrounding homeschooling: formation of citizens, transmission of values, and moral development. This is another example of the importance of identifying the outcomes of education as described in chapter 2, and once again highlights the diversity of views on the subject.

Globally mobile families, especially within the missionary community, homeschooled their children long before the current movement gained traction. Missionary moms taught their children in remote locations, while others relied on correspondence programs, such as the Calvert School (now Calvert Academy Online), when mail delivery could take several weeks or months.[8]

Today, those who work with globally mobile families distinguish between two types of homeschoolers: those who are philosophically committed to homeschooling and would do it no matter where they live, and those who do it out of necessity because they have determined that, given the options available to them in their

6. Kunzman, *Write These Laws*, 2.

7. Brabant, "Home Schooling," 298.

8. Danielson, *Missionary Kid*, 33.

location, homeschooling best meets their family's needs. This chapter will focus on parents who are exploring options and would be part of the latter group if they decide to homeschool. The former would presumably not be considering alternative options because of their deep commitment to homeschooling.

It is important to clarify terms early in the chapter. There is a degree of overlap between homeschooling and distance education (discussed in a later chapter). Homeschoolers may use distance education materials for some of their children's coursework. Does that make homeschooling distance education? Distance education often, though not always, takes place at home under a parent's supervision. Does that make it homeschooling? To clarify the distinctions for purposes of this book, I am going to define homeschooling as parents taking responsibility for educating their children at home, using a variety of materials that are selected by the parents. This may include distance-education materials for some subjects, but education is organized by the parents, rather than the educational program being purchased from a company or educational entity. The later chapter on distance education will focus on programs where instruction is delivered by an educational institution from a distance, either by electronic means or via correspondence, and where parents typically purchase an entire program from the educational institution.

As with all of the educational options used by globally mobile families, homeschooling has benefits as well as potential limitations, and we will explore each in turn and then examine other important considerations.

POSITIVES OF HOMESCHOOLING FOR GLOBALLY MOBILE FAMILIES

Parents who are philosophically committed to homeschooling often cite the ability to instill their values as a great benefit of homeschooling. In one survey, religious instruction was the most important reason for homeschooling for 19 percent of the respondents.[9] The

9. McQuiggan and Megra, "Household Education Surveys Program," 14.

Home School Legal Defense Association reports that 50–90 percent of homeschoolers do so for religious reasons.[10] Parents whose religious, political, philosophical, or other values differ from that of the prevailing society where they live may welcome the chance to instill their values through homeschooling. Please note that in speaking of values outside those of the society where one is living, I am not necessarily referring to extreme ideas. As just noted, one example of values that differ from the society is when parents have deep religious convictions but live in a highly secular society. However, another way that a family could differ from the values of the society at large is when a family from a culture with collectivist values lives in a more individualistic culture. Or, even if the culture is not strongly individualistic, the parents may find the individualistic values of international schools (many of which have a decidedly American culture) to be at odds with the family's values. Families with egalitarian perspectives of men and women may find the gender roles in some locations at odds with their own views on these roles.

Homeschooling also provides maximum parent/child interaction. Homeschooling parents and children are together all day every day. When children are in the care of others at school for six to eight hours each day, parents are with their children only one third or less of their waking hours. The desire to maximize interaction comes from both positively wanting to instill values and enjoy each other' company and wanting to limit delegating care of their children to others. If the other primary option on the table is boarding school, the benefit of maximizing parent-child interaction becomes an especially important consideration.

A further benefit of homeschooling is that it can be done anywhere, including on the go. For families whose global assignment requires frequent transitions among locations, not having to also transition to different educational options when experiencing frequent relocations can be a significant factor. For example, missionaries or aid workers who transition regularly between a base location and a remote area may find the mobility of homeschooling helpful. Business people and others whose assignments change

10. Schmidt, "Parents Homeschool," 83–84.

every twelve to twenty-four months may also like the flexibility of homeschooling, since they can just pick up and go when the assignment changes without waiting for a school term to end or needing to find a new school.

When a family homeschools, they can determine the best teaching and learning experiences (in other words, the curriculum) for their children. Learning can be individualized and students can move at their own pace. Students who are particularly interested or talented in an area can explore it with more depth. Those who struggle can receive personalized help from the parent and not feel the pressure to "keep up" with the rest of a class.

One curricular benefit that is especially relevant in the global context is that families can teach their children about both their home and host cultures while homeschooling. In chapter 2, I noted that ideally, globally mobile children will come to appreciate and value both the home and host cultures. Educational settings such as international schools may lean toward the home culture (although this depends on the school and one's home culture), and the host-country schools will definitely present the host culture but will not help the student learn about her home culture's history and values beyond possibly limited survey-level study. Homeschooling provides a way for parents to potentially experience the best of both home and host culture in a way that no other option may be able to provide.

A final benefit is that many homeschooling families complete their studies in less time than a typical "school day," leaving time for children to be involved in other enriching activities.[11] One of the wonderful benefits of a globally mobile childhood is the opportunity to visit places and enjoy experiences that would never be possible if a family only lived in their homeland. Though any globally mobile family can travel and see sights within and around their global location, homeschoolers may have more time to explore museums and cultural sites, and to do this with a depth that might not be possible if they were enrolled in a traditional school.

11. Bell, *Ultimate Guide*, 41–42. In Mutchler's research, families reported spending sixteen to twenty or more hours weekly in homeschool studies (Mutchler, "Key Factors").

POTENTIAL LIMITATIONS

Every educational option discussed in this book has benefits and potential limitations, and homeschooling is no exception. In fact, for homeschooling, I will discuss the shadow side of every benefit described in the previous section. Each benefit, for all the positive outcomes that may result from it, also has potential limitations.

Though homeschooling allows parents to instill their values in their children, it is possible that homeschooled children may have limited exposure to other values. An illustrative, though admittedly extreme, situation is described by Westover in her memoir. Her "survivalist" parents led the family in preparing "for the end of the world by stockpiling home-canned peaches and sleeping with her 'head-for-the hills' bag. . . . Her father distrusted the medical establishment, so Tara never saw a doctor or nurse. Gashes and concussions, even burns from explosions were all treated at home with herbalism. The family was so isolated from mainstream society that there was no one to ensure the children received an education, and no one to intervene when an older brother became violent."[12] Because of the family's perception of modesty, Westover had to wear a sweatshirt-styled dance costume for her recital as an eleven-year-old, but her father still viewed it as "jumping about like whores in the Lord's house."[13]

Further, though it is important that children learn certain values from their parents, be they cultural, spiritual, or other, it is also important for children to learn to thoughtfully and respectfully engage in an age-appropriate way with those who hold different viewpoints. Homeschooling does not necessarily mean that children will be unable to engage with others whose values differ, but parents who choose to homeschool need to identify ways to help their children encounter other perspectives, interact appropriately, and think critically about them.

One of the responses I sometimes hear when talking with families about educational options is "I'm not sure I would want to be around my kids all day every day." The shadow side of the benefit

12. Westover, *Educated*, dust jacket.
13. Westover, *Educated*, 81.

of maximum parent-child interaction is maximum parent-child interaction. For some parents, being together all day every day is simply too much. It is better to recognize this and make decisions accordingly than to force oneself into a role that is not a good fit. Some parents may want or need "alone time," or time to engage in adult activities and hobbies. A parent may have several children and need to have older ones in school so that more time can be dedicated to the preschool-aged child(ren) in the family. One colleague shared with me that she homeschooled her children at one point but was not very successful at it. This surprised me, since this colleague is an excellent teacher and education professor today. The reason? She had two very little ones at home who required a lot of time and attention, so the time she had available to homeschool the older two was limited.

Homeschooling requires a significant time commitment by one or both parents, and this is a significant potential limitation. In a two-parent household, it is likely that the "employee" parent would have limited or no involvement in homeschooling because of employment demands, and therefore the responsibility for homeschooling would belong to the "accompanying spouse."[14] While this is also the case with families who choose to homeschool in the homeland, there are differences in the global setting. Some of the conveniences of the homeland may not be available. It may take longer to simply manage "life"–the laundry, the shopping, getting around using public transport instead of one's own car, and more. Even in locations where globally mobile families are able to employ household helpers, these staff still need to be supervised and guided in how the family prefers that things be done. It takes time to plan, prepare, and deliver education at home, and the time spent educating the child(ren) will be time that the parent does not have available for other things. This opportunity cost is a significant limitation for some.

Additionally, in some cases, the employer may have expectations for the accompanying spouse. For example, some mission

14. Another term may be used in your organization. I don't like the term "trailing" spouse, which is commonly used in the literature, because I feel it has negative connotations.

agencies expect both spouses to be involved in the missionary work; this may also be the case for workers with non-governmental organizations (NGOs), such as relief and humanitarian groups. Parents may find that it is difficult to meet these expectations and homeschool. Those who will live among a people group for a long time, such as missionaries, may need to focus on study of the local language in order to facilitate living in the location and ministering among host-country nationals. The mission agency with which I served internationally expected both husband and wife to learn the local language and provided resources for doing so. However, when parents also tried to homeschool while in the language-study period, often one of the parents (usually the mother) could not spend as much time on the language. Too often, this negatively impacted the longer-term success of their life and work in the host country.

While homeschooling can easily be mobile for families that travel a lot, a potential limitation is the lack of a sense of home as the family car-schools or hotel-schools. Pollock, Van Reken, and Pollock discuss the rootlessness that characterizes many third culture kids,[15] and continually transitioning without a strong home base may exacerbate this concern. Further, it may limit the child(ren)'s ability to form friendships and be part of a social group. One global manager with whom I am acquainted travels among work locations in his region; he wanted the family to homeschool so that his wife and children could travel with him. There are benefits, as noted earlier, from the opportunity to travel and visit places. However, the wife especially was concerned about the challenges for and potential negative impact on their children and their socialization in this highly transient lifestyle. This is part of the balance decision that families face: there are benefits and potential limitations to the highly mobile lifestyle that is possible with homeschooling. The benefits of the opportunity to travel and visit places must be weighed against the possible negative impact that a high level of transience will have on the children and on their socialization.

We noted earlier that when a family homeschools, they can determine the best teaching and learning experiences (in other words,

---

15. Pollock et al., *Third Culture Kids*, 184–89.

the curriculum) for their children. Learning can be individualized and students can move at their own pace. This is definitely a benefit. However, there are several potential limitations when parents without a background in education select their own curriculum. First, it is possible that parents will not be aware of typical grade-level expectations and might over- or under-challenge their children. Though moving more slowly through material that is challenging to a child is helpful, the homeschooling parent may not have the expertise to know when or if expert intervention might be needed, or even appropriate strategies to present the material in a different way.

Parents' own strengths and limitations will also be reflected in the homeschooling curriculum. A parent who loves history may spend a lot of time on social studies but dedicate very little time to science. Unfortunately, many adults are not comfortable with mathematics, and these attitudes can be communicated to their children. "While a parent skilled and enthusiastic about a particular subject can inspire great learning," Kunzman explains, "her dislike of (or lack of ability in) a particular subject may result in its neglect, or at least the implicit message that it is somehow less worthy of attention or devotion."[16] While this can also happen with classroom teachers, students in a school setting will typically have a teacher for one to two years and then encounter a new teacher with different strengths and limitations, which can help ameliorate the shortcomings of any one classroom teacher.

Kunzman recounts one of his interviews/observations of a homeschool family which illustrates how parents' strengths and limitations can influence the homeschool curriculum:

> Art and music are the subjects within [the father's] comfort zone and skill set, and so they receive the most attention and direct instruction. The other subjects seem largely relegated to independent study, with [the mom] checking over their work and answering occasional questions. The consequences of this relative neglect of other subjects aren't difficult to see. During the art lesson, for instance, twelve-year-old Aaron struggles with his math, which involves multiplying two-digit numbers.

16. Kunzman, *Write These Laws*, 165.

He continues to use his fingers to multiply, even with problems such as 'five times nine'–counting forty-five fingers in all. A girl mesmerized by an art lesson, next to her twelve-year-old brother doing math on his fingers— the potential and peril of the Complete Home Education Program.[17]

Finally, though many homeschool families complete their studies in less time than a typical "school day," which can free up time for enriching activities, it is also true that some families find it challenging to find time for homeschooling, despite good intentions. I have known families with wonderful discipline and regular schedules who were able to move systematically through their homeschool materials in a timely manner. However, I have also known others who struggled to be consistent in their homeschooling. Visitors in the home, the demands of younger children, or a host of other distractions resulted in inconsistent schooling and children falling behind grade-level expectations. Families who want or need to homeschool need to find appropriate ways to protect the homeschool time and be consistent in teaching their children.

OTHER CONSIDERATIONS

Families who choose to homeschool need to be sure that their children have opportunities for socialization with other children of their age. This is especially important for teenagers, as the peer group becomes increasingly important and teens prepare to eventually leave home. In some global locations, there may be community sports, music, dance, or other activities in which homeschooled children can be involved. In other locations, however, it may be more difficult to find appropriate activities and peer groups. Further, the child's proficiency, or lack thereof, in the local language can limit community involvement and friendships, even when these activities are available. In such situations, parents will need to carefully weigh options to address the socialization needs of their children. Depending on the child's age, this might even include seeking an

17. Kunzman, *Write These Laws*, 165.

alternative assignment where there would be peers or considering a boarding school.

Support structures that homeschool families count on in the homeland may not be available in the overseas location. Well-stocked public libraries are common in the United States; they may not be available in the overseas location. I was reminded of this when one international school with which I worked noted that their school library was the largest library in the country. This was not a particularly large international school; it's just that resources in that nation are limited. Homeschoolers who are used to checking out books from the library to research and support the curriculum may find it challenging to access materials overseas. However, increasing availability of e-books and other online references may help fill this gap for homeschooling families, especially if the teaching parent helps students learn to evaluate Internet resources. Another common experience in the United States is homeschool groups, where homeschooling parents collaborate. Sometimes a parent with special expertise teaches a subject or units, or the children simply get together to share what they have learned with one another. These kinds of groups may not be available overseas, though in places with a large number of expatriates, it is possible that parents can find—or even start—such a group.

It is critical that a parent who wishes to homeschool internationally check local laws because homeschooling is not permitted in all world areas. Expatriates overseas are generally subject to local laws, including those that relate to compulsory schooling.[18] In the United States and Canada, homeschooling is legal. However, in Europe and Oceania, homeschool practices and their legality are in flux.[19] Brabant notes that "some countries such as Germany have been known to prosecute home schoolers, although they sometimes permit individual cases. Some, like France, exercise strict control over the curriculum. Others, like the United Kingdom, accommodate home schoolers with only light supervision, sometimes relying on the expertise of specialists employed solely

18. This should not be construed as legal advice. You should check with legal counsel regarding your specific situation.

19. Petrie, "Home Education in Europe," 477–500.

for the monitoring of home schooling."[20] When we lived in Spain, the Ministry of Education told us that homeschooling is not contemplated in Spanish law, and our experience was that this gap in law was addressed differently in different areas of the country.[21] This resulted in some expatriate families being ignored as they homeschooled while others received visits from local authorities to ensure that the children were enrolled in school. More recently, I am aware of families being required to present evidence that their children are enrolled in school in order to obtain or renew their Spanish residency permits. Kostelecká summarizes the legal status of homeschooling in Central Europe in her 2012 article.[22] Some of the countries have clear policies while others, such as the case of Spain discussed previously, are not clear. Parents who wish to homeschool overseas may find the Home School Legal Defense Association's "international department" helpful, including its list of international regulations by country.[23]

Finally, parents need to consider what comes after homeschooling and plan for transition. For example, if you plan to home school for a time in one assignment and then enroll in a traditional school in another location, you should explore the next school's requirements to be sure you will have the necessary records and your student will have studied the appropriate subjects. Some families homeschool through secondary (high) school. Increasingly, US universities have procedures for considering homeschooled students and will accept homeschool transcripts. For example,

20. Brabant, "Home Schooling," 298.

21. We lived in Spain a number of years ago, so this may not represent the current situation; it is included for illustrative purposes. However, the Home School Legal Defense Association (HSLDA) information seems to indicate that the situation is still similar to what we experienced, writing, "The legal situation in Spain is somewhat precarious, with legal precedent which states that while it may not be illegal, it could, under certain circumstances, be considered to be illicit" ("Spain," lines 4–7).

22. Kostelecká, "Legal Status."

23. See https://hslda.org/legal/international.

the University of Illinois even provides a convenient template for homeschool families.[24]

Mutchler studied forty-three North American missionary families who had homeschooled elementary-aged children overseas for at least two years. Her study of this group identified ten factors that were keys to successful homeschooling overseas. These factors include a satisfactory curriculum,[25] flexibility, homeschooling as the mother's first ministry priority, mother enjoys and values her role as teacher, specified study area with desks or table, good relationship between the parents and children, understanding of the children's development and learning style, a regular class schedule, a positive husband-wife relationship, and lesson plans.[26] These findings, though specifically based on research with missionary families, might be of interest to other parents who are considering homeschooling overseas, regardless of employer affiliation.

Homeschooling offers significant benefits to parents who are able and willing to invest themselves in educating their own children. However, there are potential challenges which need to be carefully considered by globally mobile families. In all cases, parents need to investigate the legality of homeschooling in light of local compulsory attendance laws. Finally, it is important that globally mobile parents consider what comes after homeschooling to ensure that their children will be able to continue their education in another delivery option or at the tertiary level.

QUESTIONS FOR REFLECTION

1. How do we view the benefits and potential limitations of homeschooling specifically for our situation and student? Which benefits will truly be benefits and which potential limitations are a concern to us?

24. "Official Homeschool Template."

25. With curriculum being defined using the popular meaning of materials from a publisher (i.e., "I use Sonlight curriculum"), not the formal definition of curriculum as a "course of study."

26. Mutchler, *Key Factors*, 27.

2. Am I or is my spouse able and ready to make the time commitment that homeschooling will require?
3. What is the legal situation for homeschooling in our location?
4. If we choose homeschooling, how can we address the potential limitations?

6

Distance Education

DISTANCE EDUCATION IS FLOURISHING in the twenty-first century as technologies have made education from a variety of providers available almost anywhere anytime. In the higher-education space, practically every institution offers degrees online in a convenient format. Professional development and ongoing learning for professionals can be accessed through online modules, and not only degrees, but certificates and "badges" document learning by distance education.

For globally mobile families, distance education is yet another option with distinct advantages and potential limitations. In the past, distance learning was typically accomplished through correspondence programs, but today, distance education encompasses a variety of technologies. Terminologies including "open learning," flexible learning, online or e-learning, and virtual education are all used to describe it. The European Commission uses the term "open & distance learning."[1]

As noted in the previous chapter on homeschooling, there is overlap between distance education and homeschooling. Parents who teach their children at home may purchase one or more distance-education courses as part of the overall curriculum for their students. I define that as homeschooling using distance-education

---

1. Siaciwena, "Distance Education," 176.

materials. In this book, we will define distance education as instruction that is delivered by an educational institution from a distance, either by electronic means or correspondence; parents generally purchase an entire program from the educational institution. The educational institution creates the academic record (or transcript) and is responsible for the overall program.

POSITIVES OF DISTANCE EDUCATION FOR GLOBALLY MOBILE FAMILIES

One of the benefits of distance education is that a student can participate in an academically rigorous education anywhere provided there is a reliable Internet connection. The Internet has opened unprecedented opportunities for communication and connection across the globe. Families on international assignment used to wait two weeks or more for air-mail letters to arrive at their global location or reach their loved ones in the homeland; today, they can communicate instantly with family, friends, and colleagues anywhere. The same technologies facilitate communication and connection for educational purposes, and schools have responded to the opportunity by offering rigorous academic programs online.

A further benefit is that parents can rely on trained teachers to select materials, plan and facilitate lessons, and evaluate learning. One potential limitation of homeschooling is that parents may not feel able to plan an appropriate course of study for their children. With distance education, professionally trained educators and curriculum specialists design and deliver the education; parents do not need to be experts in pedagogy or content. Further, parents do not even need to be comfortable with the content, such as might be the case with secondary-level physics, calculus, or a global language. The teachers' expertise enables students to take courses that parents may not be able to teach.

Contemporary distance education makes timely communication with teachers and classmates possible. Instant messaging, emails, and even video conferences help students contact their teachers and enable them to get answers to questions rather than remaining stuck for a long time waiting for air-mail communication. Additionally, class discussion is possible through video chat or written discussion boards. Discussion is an important education practice that has been demonstrated to help students learn. It helps reveal "the diversity of opinion that lies just below the surface of almost any complex issue,"[2] "develops the capacity for clear communication of ideas and meaning," "helps develop skills of synthesis and integration," and more.[3] Depending on the distance-education program and time zones of residence, synchronous discussion (all online at the same time) may be possible. In other situations, courses use asynchronous communication (students and teachers online at different times) because of class members in multiple time zones.

An additional educational benefit is that with distance learning, students have a degree of flexibility with their learning, even while meeting deadlines established by the course. If a student understands a lesson quickly, she can move forward rather than having to wait for others in the class, as might happen in a traditional classroom. If the student struggles with a particular topic, however, she can review the instructional material multiple times. This benefit of replaying the instruction is not typically available in a traditional classroom.

Finally, recognition of credits and/or transferability of credits may be easier in comparison to homeschooling when study is undertaken through a recognized or accredited program. For students from the US, this matters especially at the high school (secondary) level and in preparation for university; there is more flexibility for earlier grades. For students from other countries, requirements may be stricter earlier and this benefit can be especially important.

There are benefits of distance education that are not limited only to globally mobile families; experts identify benefits of online learning in general. One of those benefits is for the more introverted, quieter learner. Fedynich believes that the playing field is more level with distance learning because everyone can participate, and

---

2. Brookfield and Preskill, *Democratic Classrooms*, 3.
3. Brookfield and Preskill. *Democratic Classrooms*, 22.

students have the opportunity to reflect before responding, revise their interpretations, and modify original assumptions.[4]

POTENTIAL LIMITATIONS

As is the case with all of the options discussed in this book, there are aspects of distance education that may present challenges and which parents will need to consider and try to ameliorate as best as possible. The first potential limitation to consider in this age of distance education primarily via Internet is the need for reliable (and affordable) connectivity. In some places, connections may be unavailable, expensive, or unreliable. Further, since courses often require viewing videos, sufficient bandwidth to handle the course requirements is also a must. If there is more than one school-aged student in the family, a computer for each student may be required to facilitate their distance learning.

Students who participate in distance-education programs using e-learning will also need technological skills. Though it seems that most children today are very comfortable with technology, with "use by young children under age six found to be almost universal,"[5] all students are not necessarily comfortable with using technology for educational purposes. In a 2015 blog post, Watson suggests that the idea of all students being comfortable with technology is a myth.[6] Specifically, he argues that though children may be comfortable with devices such as laptops, tablets, and smartphones, they may not be "comfortable with the *educationally appropriate* use of the device. It's one thing for a student to know how to watch a video on her tablet, but a very different task to watch an animation explaining a science concept, analyze it, perhaps annotate it, and learn from it."[7]

---

4. Fedynich, "Teaching Beyond," 3.
5. "Technology and Young Children," 1.
6. Watson, "Myth."
7. Watson, "Myth," para. 5, italics in the original.

In addition to technological skills, "students with low reading and comprehension skills are unlikely to thrive in online courses"[8] due to the need to read and understand more independently than might be required in a traditional classroom. Distractions and interruptions can hinder a student who uses distance learning. Some students are very conscientious and possess excellent time-management skills and self-discipline, but for others, distractions of social media, non-educational videos, siblings, and a host of other things may keep them from making progress in their academic studies. Parents should expect to "monitor, mentor, and motivate" their students and their progress in the distance-learning program.[9]

Parents who choose distance learning for their students will need to consider their students' needs for socialization. This is especially important with teenagers, who are becoming more focused on friendships outside of the family as part of their drive toward independence.[10] While a benefit of distance learning is the ability to interact with others, such as through discussion boards, synchronous class meetings, or web calls (FaceTime, Zoom, Skype, etc.), parents should anticipate that their students will still need face-to-face social interaction. As with homeschooling, a distance-learning student can develop friendships in the local community, but these may be contingent on ability in the local language.

Finally, as is the case with other options where the child is not in contact with the host culture, parents may want to consider ways for their children to learn the local language and develop relationships in the host culture. One of the benefits of a globally mobile childhood is learning about and connecting with other cultures. If the distance-education program you choose comes from your home country, it will probably not help your child learn about your host country in depth.

8. Berge and Clark, "Perspectives," 16.
9. Curtius and Werth, "Fostering Student Success," 17.
10. Lally and Valentine-French, *Lifespan Development*, 215.

OTHER CONSIDERATIONS

In selecting a distance-education program, parents should consider the program's accreditation unless it has specific recognition from its nation's ministry of education. As discussed in the chapter on international schools, there are US-based accreditors (Western Association of Schools and Colleges, New England Association of Schools and Colleges, and more) and international accreditors, such as the Council of International Schools. The Distance Education Accrediting Commission (DEAC) specifically focuses on distance-learning accreditation. By selecting an accredited school, parents will have assurances that the program meets established standards of quality. Additionally, many US colleges require that students be graduates of an accredited high school in order to be considered for admission. It is important to ensure that there are quality controls for the program you choose, and to verify that your child's work will be recognized by educational authorities in your homeland or in future global assignments.

An additional benefit of an accredited distance-learning school is that the teachers will be trained in distance pedagogy. Teaching online is not the same as teaching in a face-to-face classroom; methods that are effective in the classroom may need to be modified for online classroom use. The DEAC standards require that faculty/instructors be trained on "the use of instructional technology" (Standard VI.C) and that "qualified persons competent in distance education instructional design practices work with experts in subjects . . . to prepare instructional materials" (Standard III.E.1).[11] The regional accreditor Cognia (formerly AdvancEd) has standards specifically for digital learning.[12] Similarly, regional accreditor WASC has an online supplement to their standards, which addresses issues including how students are assessed online, how teacher interaction supports learning, professional development for instructors to help them keep pace with "constantly changing

---

11. "Part Three: Accreditation Standards," 89.

12. "AdvancED Performance Standards."

information technologies," and more.[13] Ideally, you should look for a program where teachers are trained to teach online.

Just as there are a variety of types of international schools, there are many types of distance-education programs. Many US states have developed distance-education programs or are part of a distance-education consortium. In some states, a private company (e.g., K12) manages online public schools. This is not just a US phenomenon; various countries around the world offer distance-education programs. For example, Spain's Ministry of Education offers distance education through the Center for Innovation and Development of Distance Education.[14] Faith-based options are available for those who want their children educated from the worldview perspective of their religion. Though not an exhaustive list, families might explore the offerings of NorthStar Academy (https://www.northstar-academy.org/) or Sevenstar (https://sevenstar.org/) as a starting place.

Distance education can be a helpful solution for globally mobile families in a variety of situations. Though there are potential limitations, parents may be able to address these concerns in order to maximize the benefits of distance learning in their global assignment. Families who want their children to be educated in a manner more like their homeland may find that a distance-education program from their home country provides a portable and practical solution that keeps their children more connected to the homeland and that may facilitate transitions back to the homeland when the international assignment ends or when the student enters university.

QUESTIONS FOR REFLECTION

1. Which of the potential limitations of distance education are of most concern to me/us, and how might we address those potential limitations?

13. "Supplement for Schools," 6.
14. "Dónde estudiar."

2. Does my home country offer a recognized distance education option, such as the one from Spain cited in this chapter? For those from the US, which of the many distance-education options is most attractive to you? Why?

For further resources on distance learning, see Appendix 3: Distance Education & Virtual School Resources. Appendix 3 includes a list of selected virtual schools.

7

Boarding School

As I HAVE TALKED and worked with internationally mobile families over the years, I have never encountered a family for whom boarding was the initially preferred option. Parents are not eager to send their children away from home, and for good reason. The family wants to be together, with parents providing formative input to their children and watching them grow and develop day by day. Even though boarding is not typically a first-choice option, family circumstances may change, resulting in willingness to consider the boarding option. As Krotzer notes, "One thing that most [families who choose boarding] have in common is that boarding school was not part of their child's long-term education plan. Something happened, and suddenly boarding school was an option they needed to evaluate quickly."[1]

What kinds of changes might prompt a family to consider boarding? If a child has special educational needs—be it for specialized services for learning challenges or for opportunities in an area of strength—and these needs cannot be met in the location of the family's assignment, the parents may consider boarding. Another scenario that might prompt a family to consider boarding would be when the family anticipates multiple moves within a relatively short period and wants to provide educational stability for their high

1. Krotzer, "Applying to Boarding School," 82.

school student. Some assignments may have security concerns; in other cases, families are assigned to isolated or remote settings where an international day school is not available, so the family considers boarding so that their children can receive a homeland-style education with peers. In these and other circumstances, boarding school can be an option that provides for the needs of the child and enables the parents to continue their overseas assignment.

POSITIVES OF BOARDING FOR GLOBALLY MOBILE FAMILIES

Boarding schools have long been and continue to be a practiced educational option in some cultures and groups. "The practice of sending children to live away from home for educational purposes appears in diverse historical and cultural contexts . . . The two-thousand-year-old Jewish custom of boys residing at a *yeshiva*, in which studies encapsulate religious life, survives in modern Israel."[2] In the United Kingdom, the "classic British boarding school" became popular during the colonial period, when globally mobile families (that is, British colonial administrators posted abroad) wanted to ensure that their children received a British education, which included education in the British culture.[3] Schools such as Eton College, which boasts Princes William and Harry among its famous alumni, may come to mind when one thinks about boarding school.

The origin of the "classic British boarding school," described above, highlights one of the potential benefits of boarding school. Families who wish to develop a sense of "home" or "belonging" in the family's passport country, particularly for global nomads who have lived in many locations, may find that boarding in the homeland is an attractive option, especially for all or some of the secondary schooling years. For example, US-based boarding schools will largely have a US culture and will follow a US-style curriculum, even if they intentionally seek to be international in student body or in curriculum through programs such as the International

2. Nicholas, "Boarding School," 56–57.
3. "Boarding School," lines 93–95.

Baccalaureate. For some cultures, preparation to return to the homeland and assimilate into the culture is more critical than in others. In discussing Korean expatriates, Deza and Kwon note with concern the "ever-present prospect of going back home to live without proper preparation, especially when it comes to pursuing higher education in the Korean system."[4] Borden explains, "Many of the qualities that meant 'success' in the non-Korean culture or international school environment were fostered and cultivated by parents and the school. Some of these characteristics become negatives, however, when the plane touches down in Seoul."[5] Though a boarding school is not the only way to address these cultural issues, this illustrates why sometimes families choose boarding for acculturation purposes.

A further benefit, as noted in the introductory section of this chapter, is that a boarding school can provide specialized services that may not be available in the family's international assignment. Special education services immediately come to mind in this regard. International schools have varying capacities for providing special education services, and as noted in the chapter on international schools, not all will provide the full range of special education services that families may expect in their homeland.

Beyond special education, there are other special education services that may be important to a family. Students who are talented in sports may want an opportunity to play on a team in the homeland in order to develop their skills or to be considered for college athletic recruitment. Parents of a student with advanced musical skills may be unable to find an appropriate teacher in the overseas location or a suitable ensemble in which to perform. Even if teachers and ensembles are available, if the student does not speak the host-country language, she may struggle to be successful in this situation. Students who are gifted academically, athletically, artistically, or as performers are other examples of situations where the educational services a family desires may not be available or appropriate in the international location.

4. Deza and Kwon, "Living in a Yellow Submarine," 21.
5. Borden, *Confucius Meets Piaget*, 76.

Another benefit that a boarding school can offer is "much-needed continuity for students, both academically and socially."[6] Krotzer supports "need for stability" as a benefit of boarding from his family's experience.[7] They were assigned for one year to the Foreign Service Institute in Washington, DC for language training prior to a new posting, and then planned to move to a new post overseas. However, these circumstances meant that their daughter would attend three different schools for her last three years of high school, which they—and presumably their daughter—deemed unacceptable. Similarly, I have known missionary families who were assigned to a capital city for a year of language study to be followed by an assignment in a more remote part of the country, and the change of schooling options would result in lack of continuity and instability. Boarding can provide continuity and a sense of stability.

University admission may be facilitated by a boarding school experience if the school is prestigious and/or offers a curriculum like that of the country where the student hopes to complete tertiary studies. Korean students who have studied in English at international schools but hope to attend university in Korea may find time in the Korean educational system to be helpful, if not essential. Kim reported that the Korean missionary kids attending boarding school in the Philippines in her research were concerned about enrollment in Korean university because they might not know sufficient (academic) Korean language, history, and mathematics. They also described being "westernized by the influences of studying at Western schools," and expressed that "their values and their attitudes were different from those of Koreans in Korea."[8]

However, though this same study reported that "most Korean high school missionary kids attend a Western high school with Western curriculum because they cannot find a Korean high school in the mission field of their parents,"[9] they did feel that attending the English-language boarding school was good preparation for college

6. Wallace, "Boarding Schools," 98.

7. Krotzer, "Applying to Boarding School," 82.

8. Kim, "Korean High School," 74–75.

9. Kim, "Korean High School," 4.

in the United States. They reported that the academic preparation and their facility with the English language helped them feel ready to study in the United States.[10] Just as boarding school may help a student acculturate and prepare for tertiary study in the homeland, boarding school can prepare a student for university study in a third country that is neither the host country overseas nor the family's home culture.

Finally, we note that the benefits described for international schools generally apply to boarding school or boarding arrangements and refer the reader to that chapter to review those benefits.

POTENTIAL LIMITATIONS

Having stated at the outset of this chapter that boarding schools are not typically the first choice of families, potential limitations may be obvious. Most significant for the majority of parents in my acquaintance is that the student will be separated from parents for weeks or months at a time. It can be hard enough to let children leave the family home for university, let alone send them off earlier to a boarding school. Though historically, very young children were sent to boarding school,[11] today boarding is generally limited to secondary students among expatriate families. Young people will vary in their readiness to leave home, so living away from home may not be the best option for every young person. However, for others who have the personal skills and maturity to manage separation from the family, boarding can offer great opportunities for personal, academic, and other development.

Another potential limitation is that the full cost of boarding may not be covered by the employee's company or sponsoring agency. Organizations—be they businesses, governments, religious groups, or the military—all have policies about what they will and will not cover for expenses of dependents' education. You may find that your sponsoring organization will not cover the added cost of boarding if there is what they deem to be an acceptable alternative

10. Kim, "Korean High School," 75.

11. For example, read Ruth E. Van Reken's *Letters Never Sent*.

in your location. The financial policies may not take into account that your son plays oboe at a near-professional level and needs educational resources that are not available in your location, or that your daughter hopes to play college basketball and needs team experience and exposure in order to be recruited. You will want to check your agency's appropriate offices early to learn what is and is not covered.

Other potential challenges may be similar to those described in the earlier chapter on international schools. Boarding, especially boarding in your homeland, may seriously limit your student's exposure to the host culture. Depending on your location, you may see that as a benefit or a limitation. The benefit of boarding for acculturation in the homeland has the shadow side of less contact with the host culture.

One further potential limitation of boarding comes when boarding introduces a third country into the family's mix. For example, the parents may work in Ukraine, but their teen attends boarding school in Germany. The potential challenge is that the students may lose touch with the host country and language in their parents' overseas home (e.g., Ukraine in this example), or never even have an opportunity to connect with the culture and learn the language if the family is posted to the location as the children begin to board. The significance of this potential limitation depends on the value you place on learning about and understanding the host culture and language. That being noted, like so many things related to children's education for globally mobile families, potential limitations can have the other side of a potential benefit. In this case, it is possible that boarding in a third country can offer the opportunity to add even more experiences with another language and culture to a student's repertoire.

Kim, in her study of Korean missionary kids who boarded at an English-language international Christian school in the Philippines, describes minimal interaction between the Korean students and the people of the host country.[12] Host-country friends came through neighborhood contacts, especially by playing sports, but these

---

12. Kim, "Korean High School," 89–90.

relationships were casual.[13] Some of the research subjects attended a local church and had friends from the host country through the church. Finally, several subjects "never had an opportunity to meet the people of the host country."[14] "Only some" of the subjects could speak, read, and write the local language fluently; one-fourth could not speak, read or write the language at all.[15]

OTHER CONSIDERATIONS

If you do consider boarding school or boarding arrangements, you will want to think about the following issues, which are not necessarily benefits or potential limitations, but simply other factors to consider.

Though you may not be keen on the idea of boarding, do not assume that your child will reject the idea of boarding just because you as parents do not like the idea. Believe it or not, some students *ask* to go to boarding school. Don't take that personally. They are not rejecting you as parents or saying they do not love and appreciate their family. Students may ask to go to boarding school because they are not satisfied with their current schooling arrangement: school may not be challenging enough, too challenging, or not providing something they need or want. Their request may stem from a desire to be with friends who attend the boarding school or the need for more peer relationships, perhaps especially with other internationals like themselves. This is normal adolescent development.[16] Collins and Roisman describe an "intensified orientation to peers" in adolescence and remind us that "the proportion of time devoted to interactions with persons outside the family gradually increases during adolescence."[17]

Be sure to investigate the school's accreditation, including accreditation or other safeguards for the boarding program. Just

13. Kim, "Korean High School," 89.
14. Kim, "Korean High School," 90.
15. Kim, "Korean High School," 91.
16. Erikson, *Childhood and Society*, 261–63.
17. Collins and Roisman, "Influence of Family," 79–80.

as you look for the academic accreditation of the school (see the chapter on international schools), you need to investigate the accreditation of the boarding program and the child protection policies that are in place. There are well-documented horror stories of inappropriate behavior by adults in boarding homes. Though these incidents are despicable, boarding schools, sponsoring groups, and accreditors have clarified the importance of careful screening, background checks, and having and following child protection policies. The Association of Christian Schools International (ACSI) requires that boarding programs at accredited schools also be accredited through their specialized boarding protocol. (In other words, a school without a boarding program goes through a school accreditation process. However, if the school has a boarding program, the boarding program must also go through and pass the boarding accreditation or the school will not be accredited.)

If your sponsoring group does not cover all costs, Krotzer cautions that families need to understand the distinction between "need-blind" and "need-aware" admissions. Though many colleges have need-blind admissions (meaning that the admissions decision is made without knowledge of the student's need), "most boarding schools are 'need-aware,' and if you do apply for financial aid, that will be taken into account when deciding whether to admit your child or not."[18] "Need aware" is necessary for schools that rely on tuition revenue without the support of an endowment to fund scholarships. An otherwise admissible student might be denied admission because of the student's need for financial aid. Missionary families may find that international Christian schools with a commitment to serving missionary families often offer discounted rates for missionary families.

Krotzer also points out that the grade the student will enter matters.[19] Some schools will not accept new seniors. Others may have limited seats in various grades, so even an otherwise acceptable student might be waitlisted. In his article detailing the lessons he learned in the boarding school application process, Krotzer

18. Krotzer, "Applying to Boarding School," 83.
19. Krotzer, "Applying to Boarding School," 84.

illustrates how a school might have one hundred spots for freshmen but only thirty spots for sophomores, just twelve for juniors, and none for seniors. Further, some of the open admissions slots may be used to fill spots on athletic teams, further reducing the number of slots available to the general applicant population. The lesson is that if boarding is a possibility for your high school student, you will want to plan ahead carefully.[20]

If you do choose boarding, you will want to thoughtfully consider how you will parent from a distance. Sending a teen to boarding school can make your parenting harder, not easier. Instead of being able to talk informally multiple times each day about what is happening in your student's life and how she is doing, parents of boarding students need to keep connected from a distance. Strategies include making time to e-mail, phone, videocall, and visit the student at school. These steps may seem obvious, but as life gets busy, parents may find they need calendar reminders or other triggers to be sure they remain connected with their child(ren) in boarding school. One child of missionary parents who attended boarding school told me, "It was clear to me at an early age that my parents' work was more important than I. I felt abandoned and insignificant my entire childhood, even though my physical needs were well taken care of."[21] This comment can be contrasted with the experience of another missionary kid who said, "Even though my brothers and I went to boarding school for at least nine years, I for one never felt unloved because my folks would write twice a week and would visit at the mid-point of each quarter of school."[22] It is also important for parents to build a positive relationship with the dorm parents. The dorm parents are your partners, not competitors trying to take over your role as parents.

If an actual boarding school does not seem to be a good option for your family for whatever reason, but there is still a need for your student to attend school in a location away from the family, an alternative might be boarding with a family and attending

20. Krotzer, "Applying to Boarding School," 86.
21. Wrobbel, "Psychosocial Development," 108.
22. Wrobbel, "Psychosocial Development," 109.

local schools (either state-run or private) in the homeland or in another location. This would, of course, require finding a suitable host family, perhaps a relative or close friend, as well as identifying the appropriate school and making financial arrangements that are suitable to both the host family and the globally mobile family. Though not a traditional boarding school, this home-based boarding approach has been used and is an option that families might consider if it aligns with their needs.

While boarding school may not be part of your typical home-culture experience, your life as a globally mobile family may require you to examine the benefits and potential limitations of boarding school for the education of your globally mobile children. Boarding school can provide important benefits and services that may not be available in your international location, but there are potential challenges associated with it that need to be considered carefully.

QUESTIONS FOR REFLECTION

1. Under what circumstances might I/we consider boarding? How do those circumstances fit with the purposes and educational priorities we identified in chapter 2?
2. What characteristics do I see in my child that suggest readiness for boarding? What areas concern me as I picture my child in boarding school?
3. How will we ensure that both parents remain involved in our child's life if he boards?
4. What criteria are most important to me/us as we look for a boarding school? As no school may meet all desired criteria, try to prioritize the list.

8

One-Room School or Homeschool Cooperative

PREVIOUS CHAPTERS HAVE FEATURED the most common options available to globally mobile families. However, with "necessity being the mother of invention," families have created additional options that are either variations of an option or that combine options to create a third option that fits their specific circumstances. These other options are the subject of this chapter.

In some locations, families have worked together to create a one-room school or a homeschool cooperative. This may be helpful when there are not sufficient students to support an international school or when parents desire instruction in a language other than that of the international school. As noted in the earlier chapter, homeschooling requires a significant time commitment from one or both parents. This approach gains the benefits of homeschooling while ameliorating some of the potential limitations.

POSITIVES OF ONE-ROOM SCHOOLS OR HOMESCHOOL COOPERATIVES FOR GLOBALLY MOBILE FAMILIES

By creating a one-room school, one teacher might teach all the children, or the parents might form a homeschool cooperative where parents share the responsibility for instruction, thereby reducing the time each parent spends on preparation and actual teaching. For the parents involved, it can free time that would otherwise be used to homeschool and enable the teaching parent to have more time for other pursuits, which may include participating in the work (such as with missionaries or NGOs), pursuing other employment or hobbies, or even just managing the day-to-day responsibilities of living in the location, which can be time-consuming. In one situation with which I am familiar, individuals hoped to run a one-room school with a short-term teacher for one year because the mothers on this newly formed team needed to be able to study the local language. This temporary arrangement would help meet educational needs until the parents were able to commit time to homeschooling.

Sometimes, sponsoring agencies may decide to hire a teacher who will oversee the studies of a group of children in a specific area. The teacher brings professional expertise and focus to the work of teaching. Parental responsibility for teaching is reduced, which may be viewed favorably by parents who are not ideologically committed to homeschooling. At times, a homeschool coop or one-room school can be a precursor to starting an international school. As the one-room "school" builds a reputation and more families gain interest, it may eventually develop into a traditional school.

If the parents continue to serve as teachers in a homeschool cooperative arrangement, the expertise of various parents can enhance instruction. The mom who is a nurse might teach science lessons while a dad who paints might be willing to teach the art class. The mother who majored in literature might be the teacher of reading. In this way, the talents, interests, and expertise of various parents provide a stronger academic experience for all the children in the coop in comparison to each individual parent teaching their own children. This is especially helpful as the curriculum gets more advanced and parents may not feel comfortable teaching all of the content.

A further benefit of a cooperative arrangement or one-room school when compared to homeschooling is that it can provide opportunity for social interaction among the children. In isolated areas where there is limited peer contact, especially with others of one's own nationality or other expatriates, the opportunity to be with other children can be a welcome benefit.

Finally, in the multigrade setting, students may be enriched by observing and learning from other students. Research findings from Ireland report that children who are struggling can hear the lower-grade students' lesson and can consolidate their learning. Younger children may "absorb" knowledge from the older children. They report that students become more independent because they are required to work on their own for periods of time while the teacher works with other students. There are also social benefits such as a "family atmosphere" and interactions with children of various ages. Should a child need to repeat content or even a grade level, there is less stigma because all remain in the same classroom.[1]

POTENTIAL LIMITATIONS

While pooling resources to effectively homeschool children in a location may be a good solution, there are potential challenges or limitations to address. For example, there may be parents who want to participate in the homeschool coop but who do not have the time or expertise to share in the teaching. How should the group respond to this situation? Additionally, someone will have to oversee the administrative details of who teaches when and for how long if the group is larger or more formal than, for example, two moms agreeing to trade off subjects. Parents who consider a homeschool cooperative need to be willing to take on significant teaching and administrative responsibilities.

1. Mulryan-Kyne, "Teaching and Learning," 5–19.

If an organization or agency decides to recruit a teacher to work in a one-room school situation, responsibilities and expectations for the teacher need to be clear. Is the educator expected to only teach or will the teacher be expected to keep the classroom clean? Who will oversee the children when the teacher takes a lunch break or has planning time? Additionally, to whom does the teacher go when a significant challenge arises, such as a disagreement with parents over how to work with their child? How will the teacher be supported and held accountable as a professional? Even in a relatively informal one-room school setting, there will be administrative details that must be handled in a professional, responsible way.

Further, it takes a unique teacher to work in the professionally isolated situation of a one-room school and to be able to teach multiple subjects and grade levels effectively. An ideal teacher would have experience in multiple grade levels and a proven track record as an effective teacher, though these kinds of teachers may be difficult to recruit because they are well-established in positions in public or private schools in their homeland. Naturally, highly experienced teachers would typically expect higher pay than an inexperienced teacher, and this may be another consideration for a group that considers hiring a teacher for a one-room school. It may be easier to identify and recruit a recent college graduate who is interested in a global experience prior to "settling down," but the opportunity cost of this potentially easier-to-find teacher is lack of experience and presumably a need for greater support and mentoring. Regardless of prior teaching experience, meeting the needs of multiple students at multiple grade levels in a one-room school can be exhausting, so arrangements must include provision for teacher rest and recreation.

As noted in the previous paragraphs, teaching in a multigrade setting can be challenging, whether it is parents teaching in a homeschool coop or an experienced educator leading a one-room school. Most of the teachers in Mulryan's research said they did not have enough time to spend with each grade in each subject. They reported challenges keeping all levels on task, as well as in avoiding repetition and omissions over multiple years. (In this research, students were with the same teacher for four years.) They emphasized that multigrade classroom teachers need time to plan and organize for instruction and, even with that planning time, they still find that it can be difficult to teach all or even parts of the groups together. Discipline and classroom-management issues are of particular concern, since teachers' attention is typically focused on a part of the class at one time and it is challenging to keep all students on task. Finally, the teachers in this sample wondered if spending four years with the same teacher is potentially negative to students, given that every teacher has limitations as well as strengths.[2]

In addition to the pedagogical and administrative challenges described, students may experience challenges in the multigrade setting of a homeschool coop or one-room school. Students are expected to work fairly independently much of the time. While this may work well for some students, it may be a great challenge for others. Executive function (defined as the "higher cognitive processes necessary for the voluntary control of thought and action") develops slowly throughout childhood, reaching a peak in early adulthood.[3] Children will vary in their ability to maintain focus, control their behavior, and progress, and those who are neurologically diverse (such as those with Attention Deficit Disorder) may especially struggle because of less active supervision by the teacher and increased "distraction" because of the interesting things the other grade-level students are doing.

OTHER CONSIDERATIONS

In addition to one-room schools or homeschool cooperatives, families or their agencies have developed other options. One example would be functioning as an extension of a school. If there is an international school that is willing to work with you, it might be possible to follow their curriculum,[4] use textbooks from the school, and consult with teachers from the school for support. Perhaps the

2. Mulryan-Kyne, "Teaching and Learning," 5–19.

3. Jacques and Marcovitch, "Development of Executive Function," 431.

4. With curriculum being defined as course of study, not the textbooks. The textbooks support the curriculum.

school would let your student sit in on classes at the international school when you are nearby, such as for a family living in a rural area that goes to the capital city periodically. Christian Academy in Japan has the well-developed School Support Services program that provides this service to missionary families. This sort of flexibility can provide professional support and input to the parents while keeping the children at home. The school may be willing to provide an academic record such as report cards and/or a transcript.

Another variation was developed by the Summer Institute of Linguistics (SIL). Their literacy and translation work is largely carried out in tribal areas. SIL families often homeschool in these situations. The model they developed used an itinerant teacher who rotated among the families in a geographic area, providing support and assistance to the homeschooling parent. Their model includes periodic classes at the central base when families come in from the rural areas, and families homeschooling when out in the rural areas. This creative solution tries to balance multiple desired outcomes, such as keeping children with their families as long as possible (instead of boarding school), providing professional support, and offering socialization opportunities. However, the itinerant teacher needs to be a special kind of person who is willing to travel extensively and live in various locations temporarily. Like the teachers in one-room schools, the teacher needs to be comfortable teaching multiple grade levels and subjects; an experienced teacher is preferable to a recent graduate if possible.

The variations of homeschooling described in this chapter may help families in certain circumstances. Globally mobile parents are often creative in developing approaches that will best serve their children. Identifying the best option for a family requires an understanding of their goals for education (see earlier chapter), and careful consideration of what is practical and possible in their specific location.

QUESTIONS FOR REFLECTION

1. If I do not have the time or inclination to homeschool but that seems to be the best option in my setting, can I commit the time and energy to make a homeschool cooperative successful? What can I contribute and what might I hope others would bring to the endeavor?

2. Though getting a teacher to work with the children may seem like a great solution to free parents from homeschooling, what specific challenges might we face in our location and how would we propose to address those challenges appropriately?

9

Special Educational Needs

Previous chapters have examined educational options from a broad perspective. As parents consider options, they know that all students have their own unique gifting and challenges, and they will consider their individual child's strengths, needs, and personality in selecting an educational option overseas. This chapter, however, considers the situation of families who have a child or children who is/are neurologically diverse[1] or who have physical disabilities. Physical disabilities include, for example, issues of physical access (are the school buildings accessible to a student with a walker or wheelchair?) and/or access to learning with support for visual or hearing impairment.

Educators in all of the options described earlier will hopefully use inclusive approaches such as universal design for learning (UDL)[2] and placing students in the least restrictive environment so

1. Lexico defines this as "the range of differences in individual brain function and behavioral traits, regarded as part of normal variation in the human population" ("Neurodiversity"). Wright and Owiny describe neurodiversity as a "variation of human wiring rather than a disease" (Wright and Owiny, "Special Needs," 86).

2. "Universal design for learning (UDL) is a framework to improve and optimize teaching and learning for all people based on scientific insights into how humans learn" ("About Universal Design for Learning," lines 1–2). UDL strategies include multiple means of engaging learners, multiple ways of representing (presenting) content, and multiple ways for students to express what they know.

that students with special needs can be included in the regular class-room with as few limitations or restrictions as possible. Reasonable accommodations (adjustments that meet the student's needs without substantially changing the nature of the work) are possible in regular classrooms; accommodations include extended time to complete assignments, a more private or quieter place to work, and wearing headphones to minimize distractions. Teacher education programs typically prepare teachers to make these adjustments so that students can be successful in the mainstream classroom.

However, these strategies may not be enough for some children's needs. These children may require support from a trained special educator. Parents of children with special educational needs will find that, unlike government-funded schools in the homeland, special educational services may not be provided by the school or other educational service provider or may only be available at additional cost in the global setting. Examples of special educational needs include physical or mental disabilities and students who are at the significant or moderate level on a spectrum (such as with autism or learning disabilities). International schools do not always have the resources to meet special educational needs.

For families who already have children before going overseas, mission agencies are increasingly evaluating the entire family for service.[3] This may include evaluation of special educational needs if there is an indication of possible need, since testing or evaluation services may not be available overseas. Grappo recommends a complete evaluation before going abroad, which is usually a medical or psycho-educational evaluation, or an individual education plan (IEP) if the student is in a US public school.[4] If a family is aware of special educational needs and has an educational plan that outlines the services the child will need, parents can evaluate options to see if it will be possible to meet the child's needs at the global location.

When families are already living overseas and begin to wonder if there might be special educational needs, they may be able to locate resources in some places. Rusk references a school in Tokyo

3. Gingrich, "Assessing Families," 329–47.
4. Grappo, "Special Needs Child Overseas," lines 7–8.

for foreign children with significant special needs.[5] In major cities, it may be possible to find psychologists or other medical personnel who can complete educational assessments. Expense and language may limit the applicability of this option, however. There are also organizations, such as SHARE Education Services, that offer testing services to families in their region. Even with appropriate testing, learning that your child has special educational needs is challenging. Karen Wolters, a regional educational consultant, notes, "The journey from realizing there is a problem to receiving a diagnosis can be a very stressful time."[6] Families will need support and encouragement and should seek those who can literally or metaphorically walk alongside them as they learn about and prepare to meet their child's special educational needs.

When families who have children with special needs are assigned or "called"[7] to serve globally, they will need to take active steps to ensure their child/children get the special services they need. According to Grappo, the "common thread" in the stories of parents of children with special needs is that "successful children are the ones with parents who steadfastly and proactively advocate for their child and never give up."[8]

Andrea Rusk, formerly a special-needs coordinator at Morrison Academy in Taiwan, recommends that parents think about these things as they consider how to respond to and address special educational needs:

1. Consider the type and level of the disability. A mild disability with a high possibility of progress is more easily addressed overseas than a more significant need that will require greater resources, which may be harder to find.

5. Rusk, "Children with Disabilities," 8.

6. Wolters, "Suggestions," line 7.

7. Religious workers, such as missionaries, will express their overseas work as fulfilling a calling from God. Those who serve in the military or diplomatic corps may also have a sense of "calling" to a higher purpose, such as serving their country.

8. Grappo, "Special Needs Child Overseas," lines 51–52.

2. Think about the work assignment and its goal. Rusk advises that "if a family is hoping to work with tribal groups, placing a child with extreme medical concerns in an area without adequate medical care can be harmful to the child."[9] Further, consider whether both parents have work-related goals or if one will be available to be the primary caregiver. Caregiving can be more stressful when there are special educational needs.

3. Identify what is available where the family will be working. Larger cities may have more resources, and larger international schools or international Christian schools are likely to have more resources. The host-country schools may not be a good idea if the language of the schools differs from the child's language, since school difficulties can be compounded by language difficulties. Further, school personnel may struggle to distinguish difficulties that are a result of second-language issues from special educational needs.

4. Distinguish between long- and short-term disabilities. If the child can learn coping skills fairly quickly, an overseas assignment may not be hindered. However, if the need will be long-term and require significant instruction for the student to cope with basic life skills, there may be a significant impact on the family, coworkers and sending organization.

5. Consider the child's age. It is easier to provide for young children with disabilities at home. However, as they grow and mature, needs change; children with significant impairments may require instruction in basic life skills as well as job training that may be more effectively provided in the homeland.

6. Address the financial implications. If and when special services are available, families should anticipate paying additional fees for programs such as resource teachers or tutoring. This is true even in international Christian schools that are missionally committed to serving missionary families. Children may also need speech, physical, and/or occupational therapists, so both availability and cost need to be considered. If not covered

9. Rusk, "Children with Disabilities," 8.

by the sending company or organization, these costs may be prohibitive. In the United States, these services are typically available in the public school for no additional charge. The family or agency may decide that the "cost of all these services outweighs the benefit of placing or retaining a family" overseas.[10]

7. Consider the recommendations of specialists. Educational and medical personnel who evaluate the child will have a good understanding of the child's needs and should be able to outline the services that will be required for the child to maximize his or her potential. Parents and their company or sending agency need to assess whether those services are or will be available in the proposed place of overseas residence.

8. Be open to embracing a different season professionally. It is hard to learn that your child has special educational needs, and it may add more challenge if the family needs to move to a different location, type of work, or ministry to accommodate the child's educational needs. Such a change might be for a short time or an extended period. However, families with a special-needs child must prioritize caring for that child in the best way possible. Rusk writes to educational consultants and agency representatives, "If a child's needs are too significant, or the situation is or becomes too intense, it may not be reasonable or possible to accommodate his or her needs on the field. Be willing to say no to certain requests or families whose needs would be too overwhelming."[11] Parents need to be willing to listen, accept counsel, and submit to the direction of those in authority, such as leadership in their company or agency. They may have more objectivity and can help you by making a decision that you would find hard to make on your own.[12]

Moving a family internationally is a significant and potentially stressful undertaking under the best of circumstances. When a family has one or more children with atypical educational, medical,

10. Rusk, "Children with Disabilities," 9.
11. Rusk, "Children with Disabilities," 10.
12. Rusk, "Children with Disabilities," 8–10.

or other needs, the need for thoughtful and proactive planning increases. Parents need to realistically compare the needed services with what is available and learn as much as possible to thoughtfully consider how to provide the best possible environment for their children. In some cases, it might be better to defer, delay, or decline the international assignment. For other families, however, it will be possible to secure the needed services and have a positive and fruitful international experience.

QUESTIONS FOR REFLECTION

1. What educational services and providers are available in the proposed global location?
2. For those who already have children and are moving globally for a first time: Are there any indicators that suggest I should possibly have my child professionally assessed before going overseas?
3. If one of my children requires additional medical, educational, or other services, will my employer provide financial assistance, or do we have the means to pay for these services?

10

Transitioning Between Educational Options

ONE OF THE "GIVENS" for globally mobile families is frequent transitions. The military issues new orders and you find yourself packing and moving to another location. Diplomats serve in one place for a fixed term and then are reassigned to a new location. Missionaries, who often spend many years in the same country or with the same people group, still transition within the country and sometimes to other places. In addition to these major changes, there are regular transitions as families take home leave, and as those around them also come and go for their own reassignments and home leaves. The global lifestyle is one with a high level of transience.

This mobility means that there will be educational transitions as well. Though families in the homeland may also move to a new neighborhood or even across the country, globally mobile families experience these transitions with greater frequency. In this chapter, I will share ideas to improve the educational transitions that will inevitably be part of your globally mobile lifestyle.

UNDERSTANDING TRANSITION

Before exploring the specifics of educational transitions, it will be helpful to explore the broad concepts of transitions, particularly as they relate to globally mobile families. Throughout their international sojourn, globally mobile families make multiple transitions. Though families in the homeland also experience transitions, for globally mobile families, transitions are generally more frequent and more intense due to the dramatic changes involved when moving between nations, cultures, and languages.

Most models have at least three steps or phases in transition. For example, Bridges identifies these three steps:

1. Ending, losing, and letting go
2. The neutral zone
3. The new beginning

Stage one is the beginning of transition when people may feel resistance and emotional upheaval because they are letting go of something with which they are comfortable. In the second stage, people are in the midst of the change and may feel confused, uncertain, and impatient. This phase is the bridge between the old and the new, where one is still attached to the old but trying to adapt to the new. Bridges' third stage is when the person has begun to embrace the change and is building the skills and relationships to work successfully in the new system. Though Bridges wrote for an audience of businesses and in relationship to business transition, the three stages can be applicable to other kinds of transitions.[1]

Dave Pollock developed and presented a five-step transition model, which is described at length in the book that many call the "TCK Bible" because of its comprehensive information regarding the entire experience of third culture, or globally mobile, children. In addition to Bridges' three basic stages, Pollock adds the involvement and reengagement stages, highlighting the normal state for people who are not actively in transition. In brief, the five stages of Pollock's model are:

1. Bridges, *Managing Transitions,* 4–6.

1. Involvement—The period when life is normal; individuals are engaged in their work and community.

2. Leaving—The time when a family is either deciding or the decision to transition has been made (either by them or for them) and they begin to loosen ties and prepare for the inevitable separation.

3. Transit—This period "begins the moment we leave one place and ends when we not only arrive at our destination but make the decision, consciously or unconsciously, to settle in and become part of it."[2]

4. Entering—In some ways, this is the opposite of the "leaving" phase, when the individual begins to settle in, learn the ways of the new place, develop relationships, and become part of the community.

5. Reengagement—The final step in the process is when the individual becomes part of the new community and is fully reengaged.[3]

Radar and Sittig use Pollock's five-step transition model as a foundation for their book, *New Kid in School: Using Literature to Help Children in Transition*.[4] This book is a helpful resource for parents, who can use children's literature to talk with their children about mobility, transition, personal and cultural identify, friendships and relationships, problem-solving skills, and moving back.

Transitions—more than likely frequent—will be part of life for globally mobile families, and it is helpful to understand one's experiences through the lens of a transition model. There is great comfort in knowing that you are not losing your mind when you feel teary for no apparent reason or in being able to understand that your friends still love you even as they make plans for a future without you in the community. Educational transitions, the subject of this chapter, are a subset of transitions in general.

2. Pollock et al., *Third Culture Kids*, 246.

3. Pollock et al., *Third Culture Kids*, 234–65.

4. Rader and Sittig, *New Kid in School*.

MAKING EDUCATIONAL TRANSITIONS

A good place to start is by helping your child understand the educational option she is using and the proposed new option. In an age-appropriate way, talk with your child about the current option and why you chose that, and then discuss how the new option fits into the overall educational plan. Talking openly demystifies the process and helps the children feel part of the process (which they are), even if they are not the active decision makers. It is also helpful to listen to your child's view of the current and proposed option. Understanding the child's perspective can help you proactively address misunderstandings and possible pitfalls.

If possible, provide exposure to the new educational setting in advance. It would be ideal if the child could visit the new school and perhaps attend classes for a day or two to get a sense of what the school is like. This is especially important if the child will be attending a boarding school. Much like college visits, it is good for the student to visit and stay in the dorm temporarily to begin to get a sense of what life will be like and to prepare for the change. Advance visits, when possible, help reduce the fear of the unknown by making more known. It also helps your child have more realistic expectations about the new school or situation. In preparing for and debriefing these visits with your child, think about social and emotional concerns as well as academics. Your child may also need support in understanding procedures and expectations in the new setting, especially if it is significantly different from anything you have previously experienced or if they do not speak the language of the new school (such as when entering a host-country school).

In light of your high mobility, it is critical that you maintain an accurate and complete educational history for each of your children. Carry it with you—either physically or electronically—as you move. Don't put it in the shipment where it might get lost or damaged or be inaccessible when needed. This educational history should include, as best you are able, a record of what your child has or has not studied. Different concepts may be introduced at different times in different schools or in different educational systems.

In addition to the educational history, an educational portfolio (either physical or electronic) can be helpful as you introduce your child to new teachers either in the homeland or in a new location globally. Teachers in the homeland may assume that your child has lived in circumstances very unlike those that you actually experienced; the portfolio can demonstrate what kind of work they have done and the experiences they have had. In the portfolio, you might include work samples that showcase your child's best work as well as developing work (to show progression). Be selective so that the portfolio does not overwhelm the reader and include a reflection that explains why each piece is included. Be sure to highlight some of what makes your child unique, such as the language(s) they speak and in which they have received instruction. It might be helpful to include descriptors of what it means to be a third culture kid, where they have lived, and what they have done. These insights into who they are and what they have accomplished will help a new teacher have a better understanding of how to help your child in the new setting.

ENTERING A NEW SCHOOL

For transitions into a new school, whether it is an international school, a school in the homeland, or a host-country school, do your best to build positive relationships with the teachers and other personnel in the new school. As you share information about your child as suggested in the previous paragraphs, also ask about the teacher's interests and background to build a mutually positive relationship. While you want to be sure that your child's unique gifts and talents are recognized and developed, remember that she will be one of many children that the teachers are nurturing and developing. You want to advocate for your child's needs, but in a way that does not suggest entitlement or that will be perceived as demanding beyond the scope of what is considered appropriate or necessary.

It is also helpful if your child can make a friend in advance when entering a new school. It is intimidating to be the new kid and to not have a friend or ally in the classroom. Sometimes teachers assign a buddy to new students, or possibly you could find out if someone from your church, company, or other affinity group attends the same school. At the very least, try to get someone to tell you what is "normal" and expected in the setting. We had a home leave when our daughters were in first and third grade. As we prepared for their entry into the local school, I asked my sister-in-law, whose daughter was the same age as one of our girls, whether brown bags or lunch boxes were *de rigor* in the elementary schools. Though it may seem trivial, having the wrong kind of lunch box or backpack, or bringing what others perceive to be unusual foods, can be socially isolating in the school setting. One globally mobile young adult who I interviewed about her host-country school experience recounted a scary experience as a first grader when she and her family did not realize schools were closed for a local holiday, so she arrived via public transportation to a closed school. Happily, a helpful bus driver finished his shift and took her home in his own car, a happy ending to a story that could have had a very different conclusion. Her family had apparently not sought a local confidant to help them know what to expect, including the unfamiliar holiday.

TRANSITIONING INTO HOST-COUNTRY SCHOOLS

If you consider using host-country schools or an international school that is taught in a language other than your child's home language, think carefully about language-transition issues. (See chapter 4 for a more thorough discussion of these issues.) It takes two to three years to develop conversational language, the informal language of the playground and social interactions (such as 'Throw me the ball,' 'I would like milk to drink,' or 'May I go to the restroom?'). The context-reduced, cognitively demanding language of academics takes five to seven years or longer to develop. A year or two of immersive study can help a child develop significant proficiency in a language at the conversational level, though there will likely be opportunity costs in content knowledge. Younger children have time to fill those content gaps later, especially when schools review concepts on a spiral cycle; students in their teens generally do not have time to master a new language, keep up with the increasingly demanding curriculum, and complete secondary education at the anticipated age.

Having a local friend who can help you understand the system and how to negotiate it is essential for families who use the host-country schools. In the United States, for example, parents have certain rights, but newcomers especially may not be aware of them.[5] A Spanish friend gave us insights into the Spanish schools in our community. Jessica[6] recounts that her parents were not familiar with the (host-country) school system and expectations for parent/teacher relationships. They did not understand "how much you can say without completely offending them."[7] Her parents would have benefitted from a local friend who could have helped them navigate the relationships with school personnel. Note that this local friend needs to be someone from the host culture and not another expatriate. Other expatriates are helpful when you want to know where to buy peanut butter or another homeland "delicacy," but their understandings of the local culture may not be accurate. Though not school related, one of my experiences may help illustrate this point. When we first moved to Madrid, our next-door flat neighbors were a Spanish man married to British woman. I asked the wife about the appropriate tip for our doorman, thinking she would know, having lived in Spain for a period of time and being married to a Spaniard. However, I learned from our doorman's displeasure that I should have asked our neighbors across the hall, both Spaniards, for advice on the appropriate tip amount. The two amounts differed significantly, and following the counsel of our Spanish neighbors paid off in better service and relationships for us.

5. A helpful resource is Copeland and Bennett's *Understanding American Schools*.

6. A pseudonym.

7. Wrobbel, "University-Level Academic Success," 140.

TRANSITIONS FROM HOST-COUNTRY SCHOOLS
TO EDUCATION IN THE HOME LANGUAGE

Those who use host-country or other schools where the home language is not the language of instruction also need to plan carefully for the transition to formal study in the first, or home, language. Even if your family speaks the home language within the household, if your child has studied in the host-country schools, she will have learned academic concepts in the host-country language and, though she will understand the concepts, she may not have the academic language to talk about them in your home language. Students interviewed for my research talked about challenges as they transitioned. They had to learn new vocabulary, including not only the vocabulary of academic language but also slang and idioms. Esther, for example, said that terms in science "sound familiar but there's still stuff that I know in Spanish . . . or that I can recognize but I can't say it and I can't write it on tests."[8] Others described challenges with writing essays in academic English. Content was not the problem; the challenge was expressing their ideas with correct grammar and in the style of writing that was preferred in their home country rather than the host country. Note-taking was sometimes stressful, and at least one student reported taking notes in the language of the former host-country school because it was faster. Another new experience that required an adjustment was taking multiple-choice, fill-in-the-bubble exams because this form of evaluation was not used in their host-country school.[9]

Parents who use host-country schools should also anticipate that their child will learn different content, which may result in them having content gaps when they enter schooling in the home language. For example, a student who attends host-country schools in Italy may have a deep knowledge of Italian and European history but may have less knowledge about the history and geography of your home country. Though there is a growing emphasis on introducing students to literature from a variety of authors, periods, and cultural backgrounds, students who attend host-country schools

8. Wrobbel, "University-Level Academic Success," 112.
9. Wrobbel, "University-Level Academic Success," 111–24.

will likely have studied a different literary canon. Those whose home countries still cling to the imperial measurement system will not necessarily need to know how to convert liters to quarts, but they will need to have an idea of how to measure in inches, feet, yards, cups, ounces, and pounds. Parents who choose host-country schools will need to identify ways to address these information gaps.

It is likely that children transitioning from a host-country school to one based on your home country's educational system (including one in the homeland) will also experience cultural changes. Classroom practices and customs will be different. These may include things such as how to interact with the teacher and what is considered respectful or disrespectful. In some cultures, students are expected to challenge ideas and think independently, while others emphasize using the ideas of experts. Globally mobile children who have studied in host-country schools may not be familiar with the concept of plagiarism and academic integrity as understood in the United States. This is both a cultural and academic difference in terms of how using the work of others is viewed. "In [the host country where I studied]," reports one interviewee, "you would copy as much as you wanted to, and nobody's ever heard of the word plagiarism before . . . So I came [to the US] and everybody's making this huge deal about it."[10] Parents need to be sure to help their transitioning child understand these kinds of expectations and differences as they transition from the host-country schools to those of a different national system.

Information earlier in this chapter regarding transitioning between educational options also applies to a return to the homeland. Whether this change is the relatively simple change from an international school that is similar to the homeland to a local school at "home," or the more complex shift where the language and culture of instruction changes, the information about transitioning between options and ways to prepare applies. The next chapter focuses on educational planning for repatriation, including college/university study.

10. Wrobbel, "University-Level Academic Success," 145.

Dave Pollock, who wrote and spoke extensively about the third culture kid experience, said that the average third culture kid (globally mobile child) makes eight major transitions in the first eighteen years of life. Those transitions will include educational changes: changing schools and possibly changing schooling systems. One of the ways to maximize the benefits and minimize the challenges of an internationally mobile lifestyle is to plan and prepare carefully for educational transitions.

QUESTIONS FOR REFLECTION

1. As I think about the educational plan for my children, what transitions do I anticipate, and how can I prepare to help make those transitions as smooth as possible?
2. What kind of educational records do I have for my child/children? What steps do I need to take to ensure accessibility as we transition?
3. How can I help my child/children showcase who they are and introduce them to new teachers, including their strengths, interests, and needs for growth?

11

Educational Planning for the Transition to University and Adulthood

RETURNING TO THE HOMELAND after living internationally can be one of the biggest challenges globally mobile families face. In fact, psychiatrist Sydney Werkman believes that "the task of readapting to the United States after overseas living is, for many, the most difficult hurdle in the cycle of international life."[1] Further, Kohls reports that "those who have done the best job of adjusting to and fitting into the foreign culture abroad are the very ones who can be expected to have the hardest time readjusting upon arrival back home."[2]

Part of the challenge is that globally mobile people expect going home to be easy but find that living internationally has changed them. Additionally, our family, friends, and home culture have changed, too. You and your children will be different people because of your international sojourn. One of the pioneer researchers in the field of third culture kids (TCKs) and the life of global expatriates was Ruth Hill Useem. In response to the question of how long it takes TCKs to readjust to life in America, she said, "They never adjust. They adapt, they find niches, they take risks, they fail

1. Austin, "Interpersonal Stresses," 135.
2. Kohls, *Survival Kit*, 128.

and pick themselves up again . . . Their camouflaged exteriors and understated ways of presenting themselves hide the rich inner lives, remarkable talents, and often strongly held contradictory opinions on the world at large and the world at hand."[3]

For globally mobile families who have lived outside their home country for many years, the transition of their teen students to tertiary education or beginning work as a young adult can be challenging. In my experience, families will often try to take a longer home leave as children enter university in order to be near their children as they make that transition. It is understandable that parents will want to be close geographically during these important years. Some families even choose to make a more permanent transition away from the globally mobile lifestyle when their children reach this age, if possible. If the parents remain in an international occupation, they will need to think carefully about how to support their young-adult children in the transition to the homeland. Some organizations, such as Barnabas International, Interaction International, and the Narramore Christian Foundation, offer reentry seminars for the returning young-adult children of missionaries.

However, it is not always possible for parents to take an extended leave or repatriate permanently as their young-adult children enter university. Professionally, your company or sponsoring organization may not be willing to give you extended leave in the homeland or a change of assignment. On a personal level, you may find that what is helpful for one child creates a challenge for another in the family. Consider, for example, the scenario of a family with two children, one of whom is completing secondary school and the other who is two years younger. For ease, I will use the US designations of secondary-school grades: twelve (the final year in secondary, or high, school) through nine (the first year of high school). As the older child completes grade twelve, the younger sibling will be completing grade ten. If the family goes to the homeland for the oldest child's first year of university, that means the younger sibling will spend grade eleven in the homeland and return overseas for the final year of secondary school, grade twelve. This disturbance

3. Useem and Cottrell, "TCKs," lines 90–97.

to secondary schooling, even if the younger sibling is in the same school for grades ten and twelve (unlikely in many global scenarios) will not make the younger sibling happy in almost any case. Worse, this approach could mean three different schools for three of the four years of high school, causing challenges educationally and socially. This scenario only gets more complicated if there are more children in the family. Going to the homeland for the first year of university may not work in all situations.

Globally mobile parents need to plan in advance for their child(ren)'s post-secondary experience. This will look different for families from different homelands and will vary based on the family's expectations and hopes for their children. Many, though not all, young people will plan to return to their homeland for university study. Others may opt for study in a third country, such as Korean students who have lived in Colombia and wish to study in the United States. If the young people have studied in host-country schools and have a strong command of the language, they may opt to remain in the global location and study in a university there. The options are extensive, so in this chapter, I am going to focus specifically on preparation for and transition to the United States for tertiary study. This is the area where I have the most expertise, and it may serve the majority of readers. For those who do not plan to pursue tertiary study in the US, perhaps the topics will suggest avenues of investigation as you learn about the situation in the place where your student plans to study.

For students who plan to study at university, selecting an institution should begin early. Students should think about the program(s) they are interested in and the schools that offer programs in that field. Students who don't know for sure what they want to study, or who have several possible fields in mind, may want to look at schools that have all of those fields. Even if your student feels certain about an intended field of study, think about schools that offer options. Many undergraduates (at least one-third[4]) change their major. When on home leaves, take time to visit schools that may be of interest. The campus visit is an important

4. "Beginning College Students," lines 1–2.

part of the selection process for many students in the United States, as it helps students get a feel for the campus community and explore the "fit" of the institution.

In chapter 3, we discussed the importance of school accreditation when selecting an international school. For higher education, accreditation is even more important. Accredited institutions meet established standards for quality that include the educational program, systematic review and improvement of the educational program, and resources to carry out the educational program. Attending an accredited school will be important if you decide to change schools (transfer) and for recognition of your degree. It will also be relevant if you choose to pursue graduate studies. You will usually find accreditation information in the "about" section of the school's web page or if you search the term "accreditation." Take note of any kinds of conditions or sanctions, which indicate the school does not meet or is in danger of not meeting one or more accreditation standards. Universities in the US are accredited by accreditors such as the New England Association of Schools and Colleges, the Higher Learning Commission, and the Western Association of Schools and Colleges. There are also specialized accreditors for fields such as nursing (Commission on the Collegiate Nursing Education [CCNE]), business (AACSB International), teaching (Council for the Accreditation of Educator Preparation [CAEP]), and religious studies (Association for Biblical Higher Education [ABHE], Transnational Association of Christian Colleges and Schools [TRACS]).

Another factor to consider is the size of the school. In the US, students can attend a large public university with fifty thousand or more students, or students can find a smaller school, often private, with an enrollment of five thousand or less. Large schools have pretty much everything: a variety of majors, multiple affinity groups, and a large selection of student services. A large school may be the right fit for some students. However, at large research institutions, undergraduates are generally at the bottom of the hierarchy. Classes may be taught be graduate teaching assistants rather than by professors. At smaller colleges that emphasize teaching, students are more likely to be taught by a professor instead of teaching assistants. Small colleges offer many opportunities for involvement and for being personally known.

The campus culture is another factor to consider in selecting a school. Is the school known as a "party school" or for easy programs? (Easy is not necessarily good when speaking of university studies that prepare one for adulthood, citizenship, and the world of work.) Explore the political atmosphere of the campus and how that fits with your and your student's perspectives. If possible, try to learn about the philosophy of the major department in which your student will study. For example, sociology or political science departments may lean toward a Marxist view; some education programs have a strong focus on "social justice" with a distinct political meaning. These views may align with your own, or you may feel that your student will be out of sync with the perspectives of the major department. Consider how alternative viewpoints are treated and whether students have the academic freedom to think independently or if they will be required to reproduce the departmental philosophy in their written papers in order to pass. A significant part of campus culture in the US is the cocurricular activities, such as sports, campus groups, and leadership opportunities. In some cases, there may even be scholarships for students who participate or excel in these areas. Consider the climate surrounding these groups as well, and whether they permeate the atmosphere (e.g., so much so that the non-athlete will feel like an outsider in a sports-focused culture) or are just part of the overall community.

Families will also want to consider the location of a school. Some globally mobile families will be open to any geographic location, while others may want their student to select a school that is located near family or friends so that the student has those folks relatively nearby should support be needed. Having family or friends in close proximity provides a place to go for school breaks if a student cannot go "home" to her global location, and they may offer support in other ways. One of our daughters got quite sick during her first year in college; she was in Minnesota and we were in Venezuela. I considered traveling to the US to be near her, but a close family friend was nearby and generally watched out for her well-being, and this friend invited our daughter to stay with her while she convalesced. This support was invaluable for our daughter and for us at this vulnerable time in her college experience. For some, weather is a factor. The student who has grown up in sub-Saharan Africa may find South Dakota winters to be too much. However, selecting a school based on its proximity to a beach or skiing may also not be the best criteria, as these amenities may prove a distraction to studies unless the student is majoring in oceanography or alpine geography. For students who need to work part-time to pay for school or even just for pocket money, the location will influence opportunities for work. Students may be able to find on-campus employment, especially if they have federal work-study grants, but that employment may not continue over summers and school breaks.

A further area to explore is the relative safety of the community and the campus specifically. By law in the US, crime statistics must be on the college's website. Since all university campuses are populated by imperfect humans, there will be some crime everywhere. However, look to see whether reported crimes are petty theft or if there is more serious crime such as assaults, and look at the numbers relative to the size of the campus. Ask about safety measures on the campus.

One option in the United States is community college. These colleges are two-year schools that offer associate's degrees as well as vocational training for students who do not necessarily plan on completing a four-year degree. Community colleges generally have transfer agreements with four-year institutions to help ensure a smooth path to a four-year degree. As an example, my state has the Illinois Articulation Initiative, which delineates appropriate courses for transfer to the state's public institutions. Many private institutions also participate in this initiative. Attending community college for the first two years is definitely less expensive than four years at a state or private institution. However, students who choose to do that need to note several caveats. First, it is important to work with a transfer counselor to be sure that courses taken will be accepted and fulfill requirements at the destination four-year institution. Too many students select classes in community college without focusing on the requirements of their intended four-year school and program, so when they transfer, they find that they have a lot of elective credit but still have unfulfilled general-education requirements that could have been met in community college with careful planning. Also note that community colleges are generally commuter campuses without residential options. If your student chooses to attend community college first, she will need to live with family or make other living arrangements. Though there are many supports at community colleges, the absence of residential-life supports that are prevalent in a four-year school and that may be very helpful to young people who grew up overseas and whose parents are still overseas may be a significant factor in a decision about community-college attendance.

Students need to begin applying to four-year universities in the fall of their final year of secondary school. More selective schools will have specific, hard-and-fast deadlines that, if not met, will remove your student from consideration. Applying in a timely manner will also help your student get the best consideration for financial aid; late applicants who might otherwise qualify for aid may learn that all available funds have already been distributed. High school grades are important to the application process, and even more so as some universities move away from requiring standardized tests (e.g., the SAT or ACT) or go "test optional." Secondary school grades are an indicator of the student's willingness and preparation to work hard and study. For admission to US universities, students should generally have four years of English language and literature; three to four years of study in each discipline of mathematics, science, and history/social studies; and two or more years of the same global language. Students should explore the specific requirements of the schools they are considering. Taking International Baccalaureate (IB) or Advanced Placement (AP) courses, if available, shows the university admissions officers that a student is willing and ready to tackle college-level work.

As noted above, some universities are becoming "test optional." However, standardized test scores do provide a way for a school to get an "apples with apples" comparison of students since school grading standards can vary widely. If the school(s) to which your student is applying uses or requires standardized test scores, they do matter. Though it is difficult to "study" for the SAT (a scholastic *aptitude* test), it is helpful to practice answering the types of questions that come on the test. Being familiar with the format of multiple-choice tests, especially for students who have studied in a system internationally where evaluations were essay or oral-presentation based, can be invaluable.

Some university applications require an essay; at other institutions, it is optional. If it is optional, do it. An essay is an opportunity for the globally mobile student to showcase how he is unique. One TCK describes her frustration with the college application, saying, "The application forms weren't built for me at all. There were three empty pages that you're supposed to fill out with all your extracurricular activities, but [host-country schools] don't have extracurricular activities."[5] This is why the essay is "built for" globally mobile kids. Universities are looking for a diverse, interesting student body, so globally mobile students should use the essay to show how they are unique, highlighting the diverse global experiences in their backgrounds.

As noted by the TCK quoted in the previous paragraph, applications may ask about extracurricular activities, and it may be hard to answer that question if the student has attended host-country schools or has been homeschooled. Parents and students should keep track of service and other activities from grade nine onward. Though the list of extracurricular activities may look different than that of a typical monocultural student, remember that schools are looking for diversity and the student's unique and different experiences may well capture the attention of the admissions office. In the essay, try to highlight traits that are common to globally mobile people, such as flexibility, adaptability, being well traveled and world aware, cultural sensitivity, and linguistic literacy.

Paying for university education in the US can be a challenge, even for middle-class families where the parents have "good" jobs. Costs vary widely but—including room and board—can easily be in the range of thirty to forty thousand US dollars per year (or higher). Understand that the price listed on the university's web page is the

5. Wrobbel, "University-Level Academic Success," 127.

"sticker price." Much like buying an automobile in the US, the price you actually pay will vary and very few, if any, will pay the full sticker price. Universities should have a "net price calculator" on their web page that can help you calculate, based on your family's information, what you will likely pay for the school. US students should complete the Free Application for Federal Student Aid (FAFSA) in order to qualify for federal aid; it will also help the university make decisions about assistance from the institution itself.

Financial aid will be in the form of grants, which are not paid back, and loans, which do need to be repaid. Parents and students should carefully consider how much debt they are willing to take on for university because loans will almost certainly be offered in a financial-aid package. Grants will include federal grants (for US citizens) that are based on income, state grants if you are a resident of the state, work-study grants that require the student to work, and institutional grants that may be based on need, grade-point average, and/or activities such as a sport or leadership. Long-term international residents should check early to learn the requirements for residency in their home state, as their overseas sojourn may mean that they are not considered residents for purposes of in-state tuition and/or state grants. Residency may be based on things such as owning property or filing taxes in the state. Establishing or proving residency may take time, so this should not be done at the last minute.

As you help your young adult transition to university and the adult world, there are several things you will want to address. The broad area of transition for globally mobile families, including third culture kids (TCKs), is beyond the scope of this book. Once again, I refer you to Pollock, Van Reken, and Pollock's *Third Culture Kids: Growing up Among Worlds,* where they dedicate two chapters to the transition and reentry experience. They stress the importance of leaving well by saying goodbyes and reconciling any hurts, as well as entering well by thinking positively about the new situation and choosing and using good and appropriate mentors.[6]

Think about and plan effective communication strategies to stay in touch with your student, especially if you remain in a

6. Pollock et al., *Third Culture Kids,* 231–92.

global assignment while they are in your homeland. You may find it helpful to schedule regular video chats since time-zone differences may complicate unplanned calls, as will a busy university schedule. Emailing regularly can also be helpful, though it is important to be chatty and upbeat rather than demanding. Your young adult is moving toward independence and, though it may not feel like it, her reliance on others for some things instead of you for everything is a healthy step in that direction.

Before your student leaves home, prepare him to function autonomously. This preparation ideally will start long before the weeks leading up to departure for university. Young adults need to be able get up and get to class or work on their own; they also need to get themselves to bed for a reasonable amount of sleep. He will need to know how to do laundry, make food choices (hopefully healthy ones), and manage finances. It can be helpful for parents to help their student set up a bank account and arrange ATM access. Consider your philosophy of debt and discuss this with your student. University students in the US receive numerous offers for credit cards, and students may find themselves in more debt than they can handle if they are not careful. School costs may include the offer of loans, and parents and students should discuss together how much debt is manageable given the family's income and philosophy of debt. Students may need to work part-time, and they need to be prepared to balance work with their studies. Experts generally recommend that full-time students work no more than twenty hours weekly; ten to twelve hours is a more appropriate amount.

Do all you can to prepare your student academically. University should be more challenging than high school, and students need to expect that. If your student has studied in a system other than that of the university (e.g., studied in a British school overseas and is attending an American university, or attended an international school and is attending a Korean university), there may be language issues due to the student having studied in a different academic language. Your student may also have knowledge gaps, since education based on different national systems will focus on different aspects of history and may present material differently. Even the difference between metric and imperial measurements may trip up a student who has studied exclusively using the other system.

Your involvement as a parent in your student's education will be limited. In the US, students are considered adults at age eighteen when they enter university, so parents generally will not receive grade reports. Your student will select her own courses, hopefully working with a good faculty or staff advisor. Taking unnecessary courses is one sure way to extend a four-year university experience into five or six, and that is expensive. Help your student know that every university in the US will have a *catalog*, and the catalog specifies the graduation requirements, including the general-education core and major requirements. Refer to it often and use it to stay on course. Though many US students change majors in college, the later or more dramatic the change (e.g., from philosophy to nursing) will likely add time to degree completion. I recently received an email from a student entering his senior (final) year in our university who wanted to change from a business major to a pre-physical therapy major. My advice to him: finish your business major! At that point, making the change would have taken three more years, extending his program to six years and adding 50 percent more cost to the university degree. While all students will benefit from the help of the university's career center, students who are completely undecided especially need to seek help early in their program to carefully explore options and make a plan that will help them find their passion and finish in a timely manner.

One area that might be overlooked by long-term overseas residents is military service or registration requirements in your home country. It is essential that parents inform themselves and help their young-adult student (not necessarily males only) understand the importance and necessity of this national obligation. For US citizens, males need to register for the selective service within thirty days of their eighteenth birthday. If a man does not register, it is a felony, punishable by a fine up to $250,000, five years in prison, or both. Further, men who have not registered for selective service are ineligible for student loans and grants.[7]

7. "Benefits and Repercussions," lines 28–29.

The transition from secondary school to university or the world of work is a major milestone for all young adults. For those who have lived internationally for some or all of their secondary years, it especially requires careful preparation and planning.

QUESTIONS FOR REFLECTION

1. What do I envision when I think about my child(ren)'s university studies? This would include location, timing, type of school, and other factors.
2. What steps do I need to be taking now to help prepare my student to select a university and for the independence of university study?
3. Do I anticipate remaining in a global location when my child(ren) go to university? If so, what steps will we take to keep in appropriately close contact and provide support to our student?

12

Living & Thriving in the Host Culture

THIS FINAL CHAPTER FOCUSES on living and thriving in the global location. It may seem odd to include a chapter on cross-cultural adjustment in a book on identifying educational options for globally mobile children. The fact is, though, that finding an educational option that works for the family is a significant component of family adjustment. For example, Kang reports, "The more children liked to go to school, enjoyed their social lives, were satisfied with their education environment, and developed their English skills, the more the general environment of expatriate adjustment increased."[1] However, though identifying the best educational option given the circumstances is important, it is just one factor in family adjustment. Formal research[2] as well as personal experiences indicate that family adjustment is a key in the success of an international placement. This chapter will overview other considerations that may help a family adjust successfully to their life overseas.

Kang's work on the relationship between community and family factors and expatriate adjustment supports the notion that the adjustment of the spouse and family affects expatriate

---

1. Kang, "Community and Family Factors," 90. Kang's research subjects were Korean expatriates who were living in the United States.

2. McLachlan, "Global Nomads," 22.

adjustment. He builds on earlier work by Black and colleagues, who also studied expatriate adjustment.[3] Kang writes, "Although the expatriate may possess the necessary skills for successful international adjustment, if his or her spouse does not possess these same skills, an aborted assignment may ensue simply because the spouse or family members cannot adjust to the new culture."[4] Indeed, Kang found that "overall spousal adjustment was a significant predictor of the overall adjustment of the Korean expatriates in the United States."[5]

The "trailing spouse" (the spouse who accompanies the "assigned" employee) and children may experience more difficulty transitioning than the employee.[6] Though mission agencies generally interview, screen, and prepare both husband and wife for an international missionary assignment, this is not necessarily the practice in global business, the military, or the diplomatic corps. Assignments in these groups tend to be based on the employer's needs, as the employer posts an employee to a specific assignment without necessarily considering the impact on the family. McLachlan, who studied global nomads in an international school, cites two researchers who identify that the employee reports less stress than the family. They identify the reason for this as being that there is a professional network with which the employee connects upon arrival.[7] Presumably, the employee has an interesting and challenging new job assignment and connects with colleagues in the workplace. She or he has a designated role and responsibilities to fulfill. The spouse and children, however, do not.

Additionally, the norm for many couples today is that both partners work. The US Bureau of Labor Statistics reports that in 2016, both parents were employed in 61 percent of households with children under age eighteen; if the youngest child is school-age

3. Black and Stephens, "Influence of the Spouse," 529–44; and Black and Gregerson, "When Yankee Comes Home," 671–94.

4. Kang, "Community and Family Factors," 11.

5. Kang, "Community and Family Factors," 82.

6. Black and Stephens, "Influence of the Spouse," 529.

7. Maxine Gaylord and Michael G. Harvey, cited in McLachlan, "Global Nomads," 22.

(six to seventeen years old), the percentage with both parents employed rises to almost 65 percent.[8] When both partners have been accustomed to working, there may be a significant adjustment for the accompanying spouse whose career may be interrupted by the international move and/or who might have difficulty in finding a job in the global location. Kang found that "about one-third of the spouses who accompany expatriates are accustomed to working and have free time to fill. Enabling spouses to function in the host country and compensating them in some way for lost salaries and possible careers put on hold is important for retaining competent assignees and receiving effective returns on the company's investment in the expatriates."[9]

In the world of missions, agencies' family policies differ. Some make clear assignments for both husband and wife, expecting the wife to participate in the work for an established number of hours weekly. Others assign the husband and let the couple decide how the wife will be involved in the work and in what capacity. This commitment will naturally vary based on the age of the children as well as local factors. However, the connection to the "trailing-spouse" research cited in the previous paragraph is that wives may feel more transition stress as they try to discern an appropriate role in the assigned location. We were fortunate to serve with a mission agency that gave us freedom in determining the most appropriate role for me. They affirmed the importance of caring for the home and children while encouraging wives to participate in wider spiritual ministry. This was a helpful policy, but not always an easy one to put into practice. I felt called to the work just as much as my husband and truly desired to participate in it, yet I was at home changing diapers. I love my children and embraced the importance of being with them at home during their young, formative years. Nevertheless, there was stress as we tried to find the right balance and discern the appropriate role for me, the accompanying spouse.

In other cases, the mission organization may make work assignments for both spouses. While this may be clearer in terms of

8. "Employment in Families," lines 1–5.

9. Kang, "Community and Family Factors," 4.

roles, it creates other challenges. A couple may want the wife to focus exclusively on the children and care of the home. In this case, being required to work ten, fifteen, or even twenty hours weekly may feel like an inappropriate intrusion on the family.

A further factor that may impact the family and specifically the spouse's adjustment is that the employee makes the decision to take the overseas posting. Therefore, the spouse may feel a lack of agency in the decision. McLachlan's research speaks about control of the family's destiny as a factor in adjustment:

> Another reason men[10] may have less stress with reloca-
> tion is that frequently they make the decision to relocate
> the family and subsequently they are in control of what
> happens, and want the change . . . However, other family
> members may see the relocation very differently. [Other
> researchers] note that family members who are not the
> initiators of the move may feel powerless and may be
> ambivalent and hostile to the family member who is re-
> sponsible for the change. This certainly may be distress-
> ing for the expatriate who makes the decision to move
> the family.[11]

For these reasons, individuals who are preparing for global assignments as well as the corporations or organizations who send them need to consider the well-being of the family as they assign employees to overseas locations. McLachlan sums it up in this way:

> There is an urgent need for corporations to do more to
> promote a positive family adjustment to the relocation
> . . . Corporations need to employ more 'co-operative
> types of mobility' in place of 'individual mobility',
> whereby spouses are assisted to find suitable employ-
> ment as part of the relocation package . . . Progressive
> corporations have developed adjustment programs for
> the expatriate and in some cases, the whole family is
> included in the program. [It is also important to pre-
> pare] the whole family, particularly in light of their key

10. McLachlan used the gendered term "men," perhaps because all of the employees in her research were male. I have chosen to include the quote as originally written in spite of the gender-exclusive language.

11. McLachlan, "Global Nomads," 22.

finding that preparation of the mother decreases the 'culture shock' of the children.[12]

The bottom line is that corporations and agencies who ignore the family when making a global assignment do so with a known risk to a successful adjustment and completion of the assignment. The nuclear family becomes the constant group, the unit that stays together move after move. Together, they have left extended family and other relationships behind, and together they must live and thrive in the host culture or risk a premature end to the global assignment. McLachlan concludes, "The family is the stabilizing factor and must be strengthened when living a mobile lifestyle."[13]

How can a family be strengthened to thrive in the global environment? Pollock, Van Reken, and Pollock say that the parent-child relationship is "the single most significant factor in determining how TCKs ultimately fare. It is here that the most basic human needs for meaningful relationship, for a true sense of belonging, and for a feeling of significance are met in early foundational years."[14] McLachlan suggests talking frequently and openly, and spending more time together.[15] Additionally, it is helpful if the family is committed to a common goal with an understanding of the importance of the move.[16]

One part of a successful transition is attitude. Diane, the pseudonym of one of the individuals interviewed by McLachlan, says that individuals who "feel very uprooted having been pulled out of Middle America . . . and are having to come and live in a foreign country, it's not looked [at] as much as a luxury or learning experience. I think that it is hard for the kids to take positive steps."[17] McLachlan adds, "Simon, Cook, and Fritz (1990) claim that children react to relocation in a similar way to their mother's reaction to moving."[18]

12. McLachlan, "Global Nomads," 41.

13. McLachlan, "Global Nomads," 149.

14. Pollock et al., *Third Culture Kids*, 339.

15 McLachlan, "Global Nomads," 150.

16. McLachlan, "Global Nomads," 151.

17. McLachlan, "Global Nomads," 125.

18. McLachlan, "Global Nomads," 126.

A further step in maximizing the benefits of a globally mobile lifestyle is understanding and accepting transitions because there will be multiple transitions in your life. Families move to new assignments in new countries, transition from and to the global location for home leave, make moves within their international location (across a city or within the country), and, in many cases, eventually reintegrate into their homeland. The degree of transience varies among families. Some have brief tours overseas while others, such as career diplomats, live internationally on a semi-permanent basis and are assigned to new posts every few years. One family in McLachlan's study had moved eighteen times in a fourteen-year period.[19] Even those who don't move as frequently still experience multiple transitions because they are impacted by the high turnover of others. Exploring transition in depth is beyond the scope of this book. However, it is important to recognize that globally mobile families do experience a significant number of transitions and need to successfully navigate them in order to thrive in their international assignment.

Parents can help their children identify and appreciate the many benefits of an internationally mobile lifestyle. Pollock, Van Reken, and Pollock identify a number of benefits of living internationally,[20] and as a person who lived internationally for twenty years and raised her children overseas, I can affirm that there are many benefits to the global lifestyle. We and our children learned another language. We had friends from and came to appreciate many things about our host counties, so much so that when I recently had the opportunity to return to the country where we lived for fourteen years after a twenty-year absence, I was surprised at how "at home" I still felt after all those years. The globally mobile lifestyle gave us opportunities for travel, and the family was able to see and experience things of which many in the homeland only dream. As a college professor showed slides of and talked about the Bayeux Tapestry, one of our daughters commented, "I've seen that!" It was a moment where she recognized one of the significant benefits of a globally mobile upbringing.

19. McLachlan, "Global Nomads," 243.
20. Pollock et al., *Third Culture Kids*, 139–51.

There are, though, human costs to this lifestyle, and those who plan to take on a global assignment as well as the organizations that send them need to be aware of these challenges and provide resources to help address them. Again, Pollock, Van Reken, and Pollock address this in depth, and I commend their book to you for further reading.[21] Based on her research with globally mobile families at an international school, McLachlan identified six themes of human cost in the internationally mobile lifestyle.[22]

The first relates to grief and parents' sense of guilt regarding the grief that the globally mobile lifestyle brings. Parents feel guilty about the negative effects of relocation, even while they acknowledge the benefits of the globally mobile lifestyle. Their fears include that children may lack a sense of place or belonging. This speaks to the question "Where is home?" that is so difficult for globally mobile children to answer. Is home where I am living now, where my parents are from, what my passport says, or somewhere else? Our friends who served with the US Air Force had a cross-stitched decoration that said, "Home is where the Air Force sends you." Because assignments change frequently for many globally mobile families, grief and guilt can also stem from not living in one place long enough to develop emotional security. McLachlan reports that parents also fear that their children will not adjust to their "home culture," if there is one.[23]

A second human cost of the globally mobile lifestyle is the possibility of grieving children. Children do not always have the coping mechanisms for dealing with pain and grief that adults have been able to develop through their own past knowledge and experience. Globally mobile families may experience more pain and loss because of their own transience, not staying long enough in one place to make good friends or just making friends and finding it is time to move on. Even among those who stay in the same host culture for a long time, such as missionary families, others around them are coming and going, so there is still grief and loss. Reportedly, the

---

21. Pollock et al., *Third Culture Kids*, 139–51.

22. McLachlan, "Global Nomads," 113.

23. McLachlan, "Global Nomads," 115–16.

average TCK makes eight major moves by age eighteen.[24] Though I initially questioned his average and thought our relatively stable family (we lived in one place overseas for fourteen years) would fall below the average, I discovered that our children had indeed experienced about the average number of transitions due to home leave and other factors.

McLachlan's first two human costs, grief of parents and grieving children, are largely a result of what she identifies as a third human cost: transience. Pollock, Van Reken, and Pollock talk about rootlessness and restlessness.[25] Because children are uprooted regularly, they experience grief and loss, and their parents grieve over causing their children grief. Further, as noted earlier, children are left without roots. McLachlan reports, "Many internationally mobile families live in a constant state of transition."[26] She notes that this transience and its impact on relationships can be particularly problematic for adolescents,[27] whose healthy development includes increasing independence from the family and strengthened relationships with peers.

To help address the issue of roots, some suggest identifying a permanent home as a stabilizing factor. It may be keeping a house or cottage in a location where the children have grown up or consistently returning to the same area on home leaves. Parents may not need this stable place, but children do. However, it may be that roots are relational, not geographical. Pollock, Van Reken, and Pollock report that third culture kids have "commonalities of feelings and experiences" with others of similar experience."[28] The real "home culture" for globally mobile children is the culture of other global nomads.

A further human cost is to the spouses who accompany their partners on the global assignment. If they did not choose to live globally, which is the case for almost all categories of international

24. Morris, "Upsides and Downsides," lines 32–33.

25. Pollock et al., *Third Culture Kids*, 183–93.

26. McLachlan, "Global Nomads," 124.

27. McLachlan, "Global Nomads," 124.

28. Pollock et al., *Third Culture Kids*, 32.

employees except perhaps missionaries, who may have both agreed to live internationally, these spouses have had "changes imposed on many aspects of their lives."[29] Women who were employed in the home country are not employed overseas. "For many women," McLachlan writes, "careers are put on hold or given up when they move abroad. This means that suddenly, these women have a lot of unstructured free time that did not exist when they lived in their home country. In order to fill this particular gap, many mothers become involved in the schools their children attend."[30]

Another challenge for internationally mobile families is parents' fear for their children, who may be sheltered in the global assignment location. Students who attend an international school are part of a closed community, where every effort (appropriately) is made to keep them safe. They will interact with other expatriates and the wealthiest of the host country-nationals, due to the cost of international schools in most circumstances. As a result, they are sheltered. They rarely meet children from other social classes and are not directly impacted by poverty. In spite of the rich opportunities that can be part of a global assignment to learn about other places, peoples, and cultures, globally mobile children may only experience an expatriate "bubble," where others are like them and most of the comforts of "home" are available to them.

Finally, with the family being the one consistent unit through many moves and transitions, the family may bind together closely. However, McLachlan found that instead of binding the family, these constant transitions might result in a bound mother. Among her research population, many fathers were away on business frequently and children spent a lot of time with their mothers. This may lead children to become highly dependent on mothers. This is an additional possible human cost of the globally mobile family.[31]

The globally mobile lifestyle has potential challenges, as just described, as well as many advantages, as described earlier. For

---

29. McLachlan, "Global Nomads," 127.
30. McLachlan, "Global Nomads," 128.
31. McLachlan, "Global Nomads," 127–132.

most globally mobile families, the positives outweigh the negatives. McLachlan sums it up in this way:

> "The [internationally mobile] families in my study are advantaged in terms of resources and support. They have many personal resources, family resources as well as external resources available to them. They use their resources and newly established support networks to lessen the tensions of the restructuring process . . . [They view their lifestyle] in terms of being part of a rich, multi-cultural international environment."[32]

What may cause crisis for some families is sought after by others who desire the rich environment afforded by the global lifestyle.

The bottom line is that families who are undertaking a global assignment, and the companies or agencies that send them, must pay attention to and prepare the employee *and* the family to not just live but thrive in the host culture. For businesses and other sponsoring groups, this means giving focused attention to the family. While human resource departments typically do not even inquire about employees' families, the family must be considered when considering a global assignment. This includes helping the parents appropriately educate their children, the focus of this book, and more.

For employees and their spouses, a key message is that attitude is important. If you view the global assignment as an exciting opportunity in which you will experience professional and personal growth, see the world in a new light, and learn about new people and places, you are much more likely to have a successful adjustment. This does not mean that there will not be challenges or "culture shock," but it does mean that the person who recognizes the normalcy of a honeymoon period followed by frustration leading eventually to adjustment and acceptance, and who is mentally prepared to weather the challenges, is more likely to thrive in a global assignment.

Dave Pollock stressed the importance of maximizing the benefits and minimizing the challenges in his work with third culture

32. McLachlan, "Global Nomads," 144.

kids. However, his advice is apropos for globally mobile adults and the organizations who send them. Those who thrive in an international environment recognize the challenges and work to ameliorate them as best as possible; they also do their best to make the most of the global assignment. It is my hope that you will use the information in this book so that you will be able to thrive.

QUESTIONS FOR REFLECTION

1. How do I feel about the global assignment? Is my attitude helping or hurting me?

2. What resources does my company/sponsoring agency offer to help my family maximize the benefits and minimize the challenges of the global assignment? Is there anything that would be helpful that they are not doing, and might I be able to suggest they assist in that way?

3. For companies or sponsoring agencies: What supports do we provide for families before, during, and after a global assignment, and do these resources help them maximize the benefits and minimize the challenges? What might we need to begin to offer the families under our care?

APPENDIX 1

Helpful Resources for Globally Mobile Families

Expat Exchange (https://www.expatexchange.com/): "If you're moving overseas, a digital nomad, a repatriate, an expat or retiree who enjoys international living, Expat Exchange is the place for you."[1]

Expat Focus (https://www.expatfocus.com): Information and resources for families living overseas.

Interaction International (https://interactionintl.org/) provides training, programs and advocacy for third culture kids and internationally mobile families. They have a helpful booklist on their website that highlights children/youth books that relate to moving and mobility that may help parents have conversations with their children about the experiences of their expatriate lifestyle.

Tales from a Small Planet (https://www.talesmag.com/) is a non-profit website whose mission is "to share uncensored and honest information about both delights (new cultures, fascinating people, unique opportunities, exotic foods) and the challenges

1. See https://www.expatexchange.com/.

(loneliness, loss of identify, struggles to accommodate special needs) of living abroad."[2]

TCKidNow (https://www.tckidnow.com/) is an "active global community of Third Culture Kid adults and youth across geographical boundaries."[3]

World Family Education (https://worldfamilyeducation.com/) is run by a couple who have lived internationally for many years and "seeks to empower parents to make the best educational choices for their family, no matter their culture of origin or current country of residence."[4]

2. See https://www.talesmag.com/.
3. See http://tckidnow.com.
4. See https://worldfamilyeducation.com/about/.

APPENDIX 2

Educational and Related Organizations

Cognia (formerly AdvancEd) accredited-school finder (http://www.advanc-ed.org/oasis2/u/par/search).

Council of International Schools (https://www.cois.org/).

International Baccalaureate Organization (www.ibo.org).

International Baccalaureate Country Recognition statements (https://ibo.org/university-admission/recognition-of-the-ib-diploma-by-countries-and-universities/country-recognition-statements/).

Western Association of Schools and Colleges (https://www.ac-swasc.org/#!).

APPENDIX 3

Distance Education & Virtual-School Resources

Distance Education Accrediting Commission (DEAC) (www. deac.org): It was initially founded as the "National Home Study Council" and focused on correspondence programs. Their website has an institution search feature and lists its accredited online high schools.

International Council for Distance Education and Open Learning (www.icde.org): They claim to be "the leading, global membership organization that works towards bringing accessible, quality education to all through online, open and distance learning."[1]

SELECTED VIRTUAL SCHOOLS

Florida Virtual School (www.flvs.net).

Stride K12, (https://www.k12.com/). Stride K12 is a private company that manages public and private schools. They offer

---

1. See www.icde.org.

online (US) public-school options for thirty-three states. They also offer online private schools.

The Virtual High School (https://vhslearning.org/). The Virtual High School was started by a US Department of Education grant and is now a nonprofit organization.

University of Nebraska High School (https://highschool.nebraska.edu/). For many years, University of Nebraska correspondence courses were a go-to solution for globally mobile families who needed either an entire educational program or individual courses to supplement other educational options. They have transitioned to a fully online accredited high school.

Wikipedia offers a list of virtual schools (https://en.wikipedia.org/wiki/List_of_virtual_schools) that includes options in Australia, Canada, Poland, and the USA.

APPENDIX 4

Boarding-School Resources

The Association of Boarding Schools (www.boardingschools.com).

Boarding School Review (www.boardingschoolreview.com).

Boarding Schools Association (www.boarding.org.uk).

Bibliography

"About Universal Design for Learning." CAST. https://www.cast.org/impact/ universal-design-for-learning-udl#.XrVpuahKiUk.

"AdvancED Performance Standards for Digital Learning." AdvancedED. https://www.advanc-ed.org/sites/default/files/documents/APS_Digital_ Learning.pdf.

Al-Attas, Syed Muhammad, ed. *Aims and Objectives of Islamic Education.* Sevenoaks, Kent: Hodder and Stoughton, 1979.

"Apprenticeship." *Wikipedia.* https://en.wikipedia.org/wiki/Apprenticeship.

Austin, Clyde. "Interpersonal Stresses from Living in a Cross-Cultural Environment." In *International Conference on Missionary Kids: New Directions in Missions: Implications for MKs,* edited by Beth A. Tetzel and Patricia Mortenson, 132–48. West Brattleboro, VT: ICMK, 1986.

"Back to School Statistics," National Center for Education Statistics. https:// nces.ed.gov/fastfacts/display.asp?id=372.

"Beginning College Students Who Change their Majors within Three Years of Enrollment." U.S. Department of Education, National Center for Education Statistics (NCES). December 2017. https://nces.ed.gov/pubs 2018/2018434.pdf.

Bell, Debra. *The Ultimate Guide to Home Schooling.* Nashville: Thomas Nelson, 1997.

Bell-Villada, Gene H., and Nina Sichel, eds. *Writing out of Limbo: International Childhoods, Global Nomads and Third Culture Kids.* Newcastle upon Tyne, UK: Cambridge Scholars, 2011.

"Benefits and Repercussions." Selective Service System. https://www.sss.gov/ register/benefits-and-repercussions/.

Berge, Zane L., and Tom Clark. "Perspectives on Virtual Schools." In *Virtual Schools: Planning for Success,* edited by Zane L. Berge and Tom Clark, 9–19. New York: Teachers College, 2005.

Black, J. Stewart, and Hal B. Gregerson. "When Yankee Comes Home: Factors Related to Expatriate and Spouse Repatriation Adjustment." *Journal of International Business Studies* 22 (1991) 671–94.

Bibliography

Black, J. Stewart, and Gregory K. Stephens. "The Influence of the Spouse on American Expatriate Adjustment and Intent to Stay in Pacific Rim Overseas Assignments." *Journal of Management* 15 (1989) 529–44.

Blomberg, Janet, et al. "Using the National Schools Successfully." In *Fitted Pieces: A Guide for Parents Educating Children Overseas*, edited by Janet R. Blomberg and David F. Brooks, 557–68. Diósd, Hungary: SHARE Education Services, 2001.

"Boarding school." *Wikipedia.* https://en.wikipedia.org/w/index.php?title =Boarding_school&oldid=907937154.

Borden, Jonathan. *Confucius Meets Piaget: An Educational Perspective on Ethnic Korean Children and Their Parents.* Seoul: Seoul Foreign School, 2000.

Brabant, Christine. "Home Schooling." In *The Routledge International Encyclopedia of Education*, edited by Gary McCulloch and David Crook, 297–98. London: Routledge Francis & Taylor, 2008.

Bray, Mark, and Yoko Yamato. "Comparative Education in a Microcosm: Methodological Insights from the International Schools Sector in Hong Kong." In *Comparative Education: Continuing Traditions, New Challenges, and New Paradigms*, edited by Mark Bray, 51–73. Dordrecht, Netherlands: Kluwer, 2003.

Brierley, Peter W. "Missionary Attrition: The ReMAP Research Report." In *Too Valuable to Lose: Exploring the Causes and Cures of Missionary Attrition*, edited by William D. Taylor, 85–103. Pasadena, CA: William Carey Library, 1997.

Bridges, William. *Managing Transitions: Making the Most of Change.* Reading, MA: Addison-Wesley, 1991.

Brookfield, Stephen D., and Stephen Preskill. *Discussion as a Way of Teaching: Tools and Techniques for Democratic Classrooms.* 2nd ed. San Francisco: Jossey-Bass, 2005.

Brown, Leslie M., ed. *Aims of Education.* New York: Teachers College, 1970.

Brown, Roger. "Cultural Dimensions of National and International Assessment." In *International Education in Practice: Dimensions for National and International Schools*, edited by Mary Hayden et al., 66–82. London: Routledge, 2002.

Carroll, Jude. *Tools for Teaching in an Educationally Mobile World.* London: Routledge, 2015.

Carter, Gene. "What's the Purpose of School in the 21st Century?" GOOD & Upworthy. https://www.good.is/articles/what-s-the-purpose-of-school-in -the-21st-century.

Collier, Virginia P. "Age and Rate of Acquisition of Second Language for Academic Purposes." *TESOL Quarterly* 21.4. (December 1987) 617–41.

———. "A Synthesis of Studies Examining Long-Term Language Minority Student Data on Academic Achievement." *Bilingual Research Journal* 16.1–2 (1992) 187–212.

Collins, W. Andrew, and Glenn I. Roisman. "The Influence of Family and Peer Relationships in the Development of Competence During Adolescence."

Bibliography

In *Families Count: Effects on Child and Adolescent Development*, edited by Alison Clarke-Stewart and Judy Dunn, 779–803. New York: Cambridge University Press, 2006.

Compayré, Gabriel, and William Harold Payne. *The History of Pedagogy.* Boston: DC Heath, 1905. https://books.google.com/books?id=bfITAAA AIAAJ&printsec=frontcover&source=gbs_ge_summary_r&cad=0#v=on epage&q&f=false.

Copeland, Anne P., and George Bennett. *Understanding American Schools: The Answers to Newcomers' Most Frequently Asked Questions.* 5th ed. Brookline, MA: The Interchange Institute, 2005.

"Country Recognition Statements." International Baccalaureate. https://ibo. org/university-admission/recognition-of-the-ib-diploma-by-countries-and-universities/country-recognition-statements/.

Covey, Stephen R. *The 7 Habits of Highly Effective People: Powerful Lessons in Personal Change.* New York: Simon & Schuster, 1989.

Cremin, Lawrence A. "Horace Mann." *Britannica.* https://www.britannica.com/biography/Horace-Mann.

Cummins, James. "Conversational and Academic Language Proficiency in Bilingual Contexts." *Association International de Linguistique Appliquée* 8 (1991) 75–89.

Curtius, Heidi, and Loredana Werth. "Fostering Student Success and Engagement in a K-12 Online School." *Journal of Online Learning Research* 1 (2015) 163–90. https://files.eric.ed.gov/fulltext/EJ1148836.pdf.

Danielson, Edward E. *Missionary Kid—MK.* Pasadena, CA: William Carey Library, 1984.

Davies, Stanley. "Attrition in the United Kingdom." In *Too Valuable to Lose: Exploring the Causes and Cures of Missionary Attrition,* edited by William D. Taylor, 155–59. Pasadena, CA: William Carey Library, 1997.

Deza, Alfonso B., and Dong Hwan Kwon. "Living in a Yellow Submarine: Third Culture Experience of Korean Missionary Kids at Faith Academy." *Plaridel* 2.1 (2005) 45–68.

"Dónde estudiar: Estudiar Educación Secundaria Obligatoria en España." Ministerio de Educación y Formación Profesional. https://www.educa cionyfp.gob.es/contenidos/estudiantes/educacion-secundaria/donde-estudiar.html.

Drake, Bill. "Educating Children in Expatriate Environments." 2nd ed. In *Cultural Dimensions of Expatriate Life,* 21. Kindle, Cultural Dimensions Press, 2009.

Eidse, Faith, and Nina Sichel, eds. *Unrooted Childhoods: Memoirs of Growing Up Global.* Yarmouth, ME: Intercultural, 2004.

"Employment in Families with Children in 2016." U.S. Bureau of Labor Statistics. https://www.bls.gov/opub/ted/2017/employment-in-families-with-children-in-2016.htm.

Erikson, Erik H. *Childhood and Society.* 2nd ed. New York: Norton, 1963.

Fedynich, La Vonne. "Teaching Beyond the Classroom Walls: The Pros and Cons of Cyber Learning." *Journal of Instructional Pedagogies* 13 (2013). https://files.eric.ed.gov/fulltext/EJ1060090.pdf.

"Find Accredited Institutions." Cognia. http://www.advanc-ed.org/oasis2/u/par/search.

"Frustration in the Schools." *The 51st Annual PDK Poll of the Public's Attitudes toward the Public Schools*, September 2019. https://kappanonline.org/51st-annual-pdk-poll-publics-attitudes-toward-the-public-schools/.

Gangel, Kenneth O., and Warren S. Benson. *Christian Education: Its History and Philosophy*. Chicago: Moody, 1985.

Geller, Charles A. "International Education: A Commitment to Universal Values." In *International Education in Practice: Dimension for National and International Schools,* edited by Mary Hayden et al., 30–35. London: Routledge, 2002.

Gieser, Julianna Hawkins. "Academic Stress and the Transition from a National School to an English-Speaking School." MA action research project, Wheaton College (IL) Graduate School, 2005.

Gingrich, Fred C. "Assessing Families (Not Just Individuals) for Missionary Service." *Journal of Psychology & Theology* 44 (2016) 329–47.

Grappo, Rebecca. "Taking a Special Needs Child Overseas: What to Know Before You Go." Associates of the American Foreign Service Worldwide (AAFSW). https://www.aafsw.org/taking-a-special-needs-child-overseas/.

Grigorenko, Donald, and Margaret Grigorenko. "Experiencing Risk: Missionary Families in Dangerous Places." In *The Missionary Family: Witness, Concerns, Care,* edited by Dwight P. Baker and Robert J. Priest, 25–44. Pasadena, CA: William Carey Library, 2014.

Hayden, Mary. *Introduction to International Education: International Schools and Their Communities*. London: SAGE, 2006.

Hayden, Mary, et al., eds. *International Education in Practice: Dimension for National and International Schools*. London: Routledge, 2002.

Hill, Ian. "The History of International Education: An International Baccalaureate Perspective." In *International Education in Practice: Dimensions for National and International Schools,* edited by Hayden et al., 18–29. London: Routledge, 2002.

Hofstede, Geert, et al. *Cultures and Organizations: Software of the Mind.* 3rd ed. New York: McGraw-Hill Education, 2010.

"Homeschooling." Office of Non-Public Education. https://www2.ed.gov/about/offices/list/oii/nonpublic/statistics.html#homeschl.

Hutchins, Robert M. *The Higher Learning in America*. New Brunswick, NJ: Transaction, 2009.

Jacques, Sophie, and Stuart Marcovitch, "Development of Executive Function across the Life Span." In *The Handbook of Life-Span Development, Cognition, Biology and Methods,* edited by Richard M. Lerner and Willis F. Overton. Hoboken, NJ: Wiley, 2010.

Bibliography

Jamjoom, Ahmad Salah. "Foreword." In *Aims and Objectives of Islamic Education,* edited by Syed Muhammad al-Naquib al-Attas, v–vii. Jeddah: King Abdulaziz University, 1979.

Jeffreys, M. V. C. *Education: Its Nature and Purpose.* New York: Barnes & Noble, 1971.

Kang, Hey-Seung. "The Relationship between Community and Family Factors and Expatriate Adjustment." PhD diss., University of Illinois Urbana-Champaign, 2011.

Kim, Eunmi. "Korean High School Missionary Kids: Perceptions of Living in Other Cultures." PhD diss., Trinity Evangelical Divinity School, 2001.

Kohls, L. Robert. *Survival Kit for Overseas Living: For Americans Planning to Live and Work Abroad.* 4th ed. Boston: Intercultural, 2001.

Kostelecká, Yvona, "The Legal Status of Home Education in Post-Communist Countries of Central Europe." *International Review of Education* 58.4 (2012) 445–63.

Krotzer, John F. "Applying to Boarding School: Lessons Learned." *The Foreign Service Journal,* June 2016.

Kunzman, Robert. *Write These Laws on Your Children: Inside the World of Conservative Christian Homeschooling.* Boston: Beacon, 2009.

Lally, Martha, and Suzanne Valentine-French. *Lifespan Development: A Psychological Perspective.* Open Education Resource, 2019. http://dept.clcillinois.edu/psy/LifespanDevelopment.pdf.

Laturner, Nancy Pogue. *Voluntary Nomads.* Denver: Outskirts, 2011.

MacKenzie, Peter, et al. "Parental Priorities in the Selection of International Schools." *Oxford Review of Education* 29 (2003) 299–314.

Marsh, Herbert W., et al. "Late Immersion and Language Instruction in Hong Kong High Schools: Achievement Growth in Language and Nonlanguage Subjects." *Harvard Educational Review* 70.3 (2000) 302–46.

"Massachusetts School Law of 1642." In *Records of the Governor and Company of the Massachusetts Bay in New England,* vol. 2. Boston: 1853. Repr. Great Neck Publishing, 2017.

McCluskey, K. C., ed. *Notes From a Traveling Childhood: Readings for Internationally Mobile Parents and Children.* Washington, DC: Foreign Service Youth Foundation, 1994.

McLachlan, Debra. "Global Nomads in an International School: A Case Study of Families in Transition." PhD thesis, King's College London, University of London, 2003.

McQuiggan, Meghan, and Mahi Megra. "Parent and Family Involvement in Education: Results from the National Household Education Surveys Program of 2016." Washington, DC: National Center for Education Statistics, 2017. https://nces.ed.gov/pubs2017/2017102.pdf.

"More than 76 Million Students Enrolled in U.S. Schools, Census Bureau Reports." U.S. Census Bureau. December 11, 2018. https://www.census.gov/newsroom/press-releases/2018/school-enrollment.html.

Bibliography

Morris, Diane. "Upsides and Downsides—a TCK Profile," One Challenge, https://www.onechallenge.org/2014/03/01/upsides-downsides-tck-profile/.

Mulryan-Kyne, Catherine. "Teaching and Learning in Multigrade Classrooms: What Teachers Say." *The Irish Journal of Education* 35 (2004) 5–19.

Mutchler, Karen L. "Key Factors for Successful Home Schooling of Elementary Aged Missionary Children Overseas." Directed study, Azusa Pacific University, 1996.

"Neurodiversity." Lexico.com. https://www.lexico.com/en/definition/neurodiversity.

Nicholas, David. "Boarding School/Education." In *The Routledge International Encyclopedia of Education,* edited by Gary McCulloch and David Crook, 56–58. London: Routledge Taylor & Francis Group, 2008.

Ng, Belinda. "Some Reflections on Pastoral Care: Perspective of the New Sending Countries." In *Too Valuable to Lose: Exploring the Causes and Cures of Missionary Attrition,* edited by William D. Taylor, 277–86. Pasadena, CA: William Carey Library, 1997.

"Official Homeschool Template." University of Illinois Springfield. https://www.uis.edu/sites/default/files/2021-01/Homeschooltranscript.pdf.

Park, So Jin, and Nancy Abelmann. "Class and Cosmopolitan Striving: Mothers' Management of English Education in South Korea." *Anthropological Quarterly* 77 (4) 645–72.

"Part Three: Accreditation Standards." In *DEAC Accreditation Handbook.* Washington, DC: Distance Education Accrediting Commission. https://www.deac.org/UploadedDocuments/Handbook/Accreditation-Handbook-Part-Three.pdf.

"Partnership for 21st Century Learning Frameworks and Resources." BattelleforKids. https://www.battelleforkids.org/networks/p21/frameworks-resources.

Petrie, Amanda. "Home Education in Europe and the Implementation of Changes to the Law." *International Review of Education* 47.5 (2001) 477–500.

Pollock, David C., and Ruth E. Van Reken. *The Third Culture Kid Experience: Growing Up Among Worlds.* Yarmouth, ME: Intercultural, 1999.

Pollock, David C., et al. *Third Culture Kids: Growing Up Among Worlds.* Boston: Nicholas Brealey, 2017.

Pollock, David C., et al. "Transitioning Between Educational Options." In *Fitted Pieces: A Guide for Parents Educating Children Overseas,* edited by David F. Brooks and Janet R. Blomberg, 324–32. Diósd, Hungary: SHARE Education Services, 2001.

Rader, Debra, and Linda Harris Sittig. *New Kid in School: Using Literature to Help Children in Transition.* New York: Teachers College, 2003.

Ray, Brian D. "Homeschooling: The Research, General Facts, Statistics, and Trends." National Home Education Research Institute. https://www.nheri.org/research-facts-on-homeschooling/.

———. *Worldwide Guide to Homeschooling: Facts and Stats on the Benefits of Homeschooling.* Nashville: Broadman and Holman, 2005.

Bibliography

Regan, Timothy. *Non-Western Educational Traditions: Indigenous Approaches to Educational Thought and Practice.* 3rd ed. New York: Routledge, Taylor & Francis Group, 2005.

Richardson, Jay. "Cherry Tree Myth." *Digital Encyclopedia of George Washington.* https://www.mountvernon.org/library/digitalhistory/digital-encyclopedia/article/cherry-tree-myth/.

Rusk, Andrea. "Children with Disabilities: Challenges Facing Families and Agencies." *Interact* 11 (2003) 4, 8.

Ryan, Kevin, et al. *Those Who Can, Teach.* Boston: Cengage Learning, 2016.

Schaetti, Barbara. "Global Nomad, Third Culture Kid, Adult Third Culture Kid, Third Culture Adult: What Do They All Mean?" Families in Global Transition. https://www.figt.org/global_nomads/.

Schmidt, Thomas J. "Parents Homeschool for Good Reasons." Home School Legal Defense Association. https://hslda.org/post/parents-homeschool-for-good-reasons#_ednref1.

Shen, Jianping. "Confucius." In *Fifty Major Thinkers on Education: From Confucius to Dewey,* edited by Joy A. Palmer, 1–4. New York: Routledge, 2001.

Siaciwena, Richard. "Distance Education/Learning." In *The Routledge International Encyclopedia of Education,* edited by Gary McCulloch and David Crook, 175–78. London: Routledge, 2008.

Skelton, Martin. "Defining 'International' in an International Curriculum." In *International Education in Practice: Dimension for National and International Schools,* edited by Hayden et al., 39–54. London: Routledge, 2002.

Sloan, Willona M. "What Is the Purpose of Education?" *Education Update* 54 (2012) 7.

Smith, Carolyn D., ed. *Strangers at Home: Essays on the Effects of Living Overseas and Coming "Home" to a Strange Land.* Bayside, NY: Aletheia, 1996.

Snow, Catherine E., and Marian Hoefnagel-Höhle. "The Critical Period for Language Acquisition: Evidence from Second Language Learning." *Child Development* 49.4 (1978) 1114–28.

"Spain." Home School Legal Defense Association. https://hslda.org/post/spain.

Strauss, Valerie. "What's the Purpose of Education in the 21st Century?" *Washington Post,* February 15, 2017. https://www.washingtonpost.com/news/answer-sheet/wp/2015/02/12/whats-the-purpose-of-education-in-the-21st-century/?utm_term=.700b2aadffaa.

"Supplement for Schools with Online Learning as the Primary Delivery System." Western Association of Schools and Colleges. http://www.acswasc.org/pdf_general/WASCSupplementForOnlineSchools.pdf.

Taylor, William D. "Prologue." In *Too Valuable to Lose: Exploring the Causes and Cures of Missionary Attrition,* edited by William D. Taylor, xiii–xviii. Pasadena, CA: William Carey Library, 1997.

"Technology and Young Children in the Digital Age." Chicago: Erikson Institute, 2018. https://www.erikson.edu/wp-content/uploads/2018/07/Erikson-Institute-Technology-and-Young-Children-Survey.pdf.

Bibliography

Thomas, R. Murray, ed. *International Comparative Education: Practices, Issues and Prospects*. Elmsford, NY: Pergamon, 1990.

Useem, John, and Ruth Useem. "The Interfaces of Binational Third Culture: A Study of the American Community in India." *Journal of Social Issues* 23 (1) 130.

Useem, John, et al. "Men in the Middle of the Third Culture: The Roles of American and Non-Western People in Cross-Cultural Administration." *Human Organization* 22 (1963) 169–79.

Useem, Ruth Hill, and Ann Baker Cottrell. "Adult Third Culture Kids." In *Strangers at Home*, 22–35. Bayside, NY: Aletheia, 1996.

———. "TCKs Four Times More Likely to Earn Bachelor's Degrees." TCK World: The Official Home of Third Culture Kids. http://www.tckworld.com/useem/art2.html.

Van Reken, Ruth E. "Cross-Cultural Kids: The New Prototype." In *Writing Out of Limbo: International Childhoods, Global Nomads and Third Culture Kids,* edited by Gene H. Bell-Villada and Nina Sichel, 25–44. Newcastle upon Tyne, UK: Cambridge Scholars, 2011.

———. *"Letters Never Sent."* Greater London, UK: Summertime, 2012.

Wakabayashi, Tomoko. "Language and Cultural Identity: The Case of Japanese High School Students Attending an International School in Japan." EdD thesis, Harvard University, 1998.

Wallace, Leah. "When Boarding Schools are an Option." *Foreign Service Journal* 88 (12) 98–100.

Watson, John. "The Myth that 'Students are Comfortable with Technology' is Prevalent and Problematic." *Keeping Pace* (blog). Evergreen Education Group, September 9, 2015. https://www.evergreenedgroup.com/kp-blog/blog/2015/09/the-myth-that-students-are-comfortable-with-technology-is-prevalent-and-problematic.

Watson, Stephanie. "How Public Schools Work." HowStuffWorks. https://people.howstuffworks.com/public-schools.htm.

Westover, Tara. *Educated: A Memoir.* New York: Random House, 2018.

"What Does It Mean to Be a CIS Accredited School?" Council of International Schools. https://www.cois.org/about-cis/cis-icons/accredited-school.

"Why School?" *The 48th Annual PDK Poll of the Public's Attitudes toward the Public Schools,* September 2016. https://pdkpoll.org/wp-content/uploads/2020/05/pdkpoll48_2016.pdf.

Wilkinson, David. "International Education and Issues of Governance." In *International Education in Practice: Dimension for National and International Schools,* edited by Mary Hayden et al., 185–96. London: Routledge, 2002.

Wolters, Karen. "Suggestions on How to Support the Parents of Children with Special Needs." *PACE* (blog). The Professional Association of Cross-Cultural Consultants in Education (PACE), March 18, 2020. https://www.tckconsultant.org/suggestions-on-how-to-support-the-parents-of-children-with-special-needs-2/.

Bibliography

Wright, Peter L., and Ruby L. Owiny. "Special Needs Goes to Church: A Special Education Primer for Ministry." *Christian Education Journal* 13.1 (2016) 85–108.

Wrobbel, Karen A. "Don't Forget the Kids! Pre-field Screening for All Family Members." *World Pulse* 39.7 (2004) 7.

———. "A Study of the Psychosocial Development of Adult MKs." Master's thesis, Wheaton College (IL) Graduate School, 1988.

———. "The University-Level Academic Success of Missionary Kids Educated in Second-Language Host Country National schools." EdD diss., University of Minnesota, 2005.

———. "When Should Children Start National School? A Look at Second Language Issues." *Interact* 11.2 (2004) 4–7.

Zaki Badawi, Muhammad Aboulkhir. "Traditional Islamic Education—Its Aims and Purposes in the Present Day." In *Aims and Objectives of Islamic Education,* edited by Syed Muhammad Al-Attas, 104. Sevenoaks, Kent: Hodder and Stoughton, 1979.